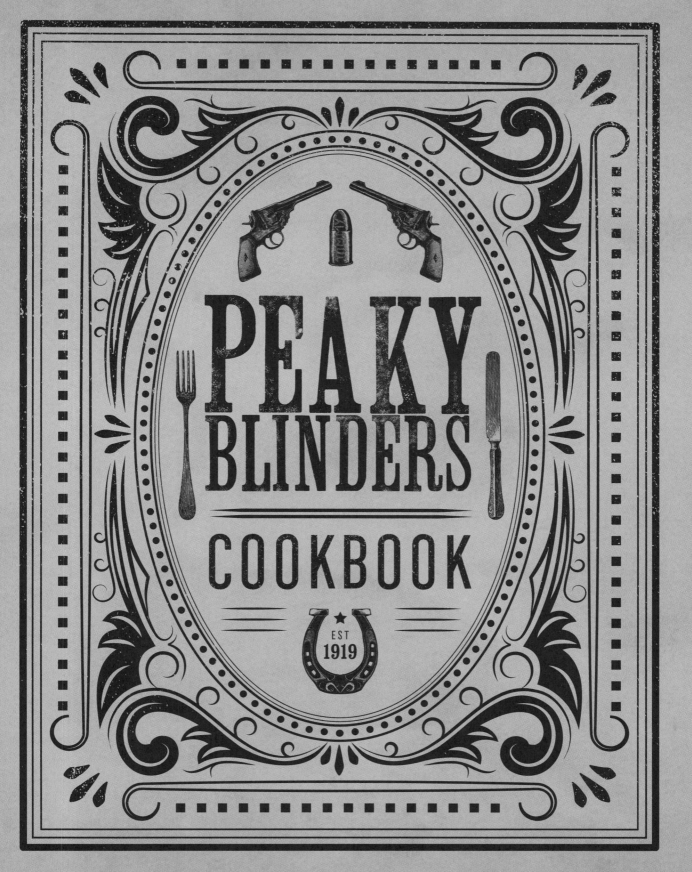

# PEAKY BLINDERS

# COOKBOOK

EST 1919

# PEAKY BLINDERS

# COOKBOOK

**50** RECIPES SELECTED BY THE SHELBY COMPANY LTD

BY ORDER OF THE · PEAKY BLINDERS ·

WHITE LION
PUBLISHING

# INTRODUCTION

Welcome to the *Peaky Blinders Cookbook*, a culinary voyage into the rags-to-riches tale of Tommy Shelby and his gangster clan. From the kitchen table at Watery Lane to the grand dining hall at Arrow House, via The Garrison, the Epsom Derby and the Eden Club, your invitation to eat with the Peaky Blinders awaits.

Food during the interwar years was an interesting combination of post-war thriftiness and heady decadence. Ingredients that today we might consider luxury or specialist, such as oysters, were far more commonplace than they are now. Chicken, on the other hand, a humble Sunday lunch staple in 21st-century Britain, used to be a sophisticated addition to the dinner table. Rabbit, pigeon and other game, along with herbs, mushrooms and berries, which were easily hunted or foraged, filled plates and stomachs even for the lower classes. Generally, meat featured heavily in the diets of 1920s' Britons – and for obvious reasons, nothing was wasted. Once post-war rationing ended in 1920, sugar and flour, along with butter, milk and other dairy gradually became more available again – satisfying sweet tooths in cakes, pastries, jellies and puddings.

All the while, among the upper classes at least, a hedonistic sense of freedom from the horrors of war took hold. Champagne and gin cocktails flowed, and canapés and fine foods became a marker of higher social class. It's against this backdrop to the story of the Peaky Blinders that the recipes in this book draw you deeper into the Shelbys' world. This is a collection of dishes inspired by those likely to have been on the table at each stage in Tommy's social climb from Watery Lane to Arrow House. Each has been modernized for today's palates, but is rooted firmly in the era of your favourite series.

# EAT THEM WELL & ENJOY!
# BY ORDER OF THE PEAKY BLINDERS...

# FAMILY TABLE AT WATERY LANE

# WARMING VEGETABLE & BARLEY SOUP WITH ALFIE SOLOMONS' SODA BREAD

SERVES **6** | TOTAL TIME TO MAKE **01** HOUR **30** MINS

## FOR THE SODA BREAD

175g/6oz/1⅓ cups plain
    (all-purpose) flour
175g/6oz/1⅓ cups wholemeal
    (wholewheat) flour
1 teaspoon bicarbonate of (baking) soda
1 teaspoon salt
1 teaspoon caster (superfine) sugar
50g/1¾oz mature Cheddar, grated
1 spring onion (scallion),
    finely chopped
25g/1oz sunflower seeds
300ml/10½fl oz/1¼ cups buttermilk
1 tablespoon runny honey, warmed

## FOR THE SOUP

50g/1¾oz/3½ tablespoons butter
1 large onion, finely chopped
2 carrots, peeled and thinly sliced
2 celery stalks, roughly chopped
2 garlic cloves, chopped
1 small leek, thinly sliced
2 turnips (rutabagas), peeled and
    roughly chopped
1 teaspoon plain (all-purpose) flour
1 litre/35fl oz/generous 4 cups
    vegetable stock (or chicken
    or beef stock, if you prefer)
4–5 dashes of Worcestershire sauce,
    to taste
100g/3½oz/generous ½ cup
    pearl barley
1 bay leaf
2 thyme sprigs
25g/1oz kale, roughly chopped
salt and ground black pepper

**We all know Alfie's 'bakery' is not really the kind of place where you would buy a loaf of bread, but what better smokescreen to inspire a simple, hearty loaf to go with this warming soup.**

First, make the bread – a couple of hours ahead is fine, but this loaf is best eaten on the day. Preheat your oven to 200°C/180°C fan/400°F/Gas 6 and line a baking sheet with baking paper.

In a large bowl, add the flours, bicarbonate of soda, salt and sugar and mix well. Stir in the cheese, spring onion and all but 1 tablespoon of the sunflower seeds. Make a well in the centre, add three quarters of the buttermilk and, using the handle of a wooden spoon, stir to incorporate the flour and form a soft, but not sticky dough. Add a little more buttermilk if needed, but you may not need it all. Try not to over-mix as this can make the bread heavy and dense.

Tip out the dough on to a lightly floured surface and, with floured hands, shape it into a ball. Lightly press the dough down to flatten it a little. Using a sharp knife, score a cross into the top about 2.5cm/1in deep. Transfer the loaf to the lined baking sheet and bake it for 30 minutes, then remove it from the oven. Brush the top with the warm honey, scatter over the remaining sunflower seeds and bake for a further 5 minutes, until golden and the loaf sounds hollow when tapped on the base. Leave to cool.

While the bread is cooling, make the soup. Melt the butter in a large saucepan or casserole over a low–medium heat. Add the onion, carrots, celery, garlic, leek and turnips, put the lid on the pan and cook for about 10 minutes, until softened but not browned.

Remove the lid and mix in the flour, then pour in the stock and Worcestershire sauce. Bring the liquid to a simmer. Add the pearl barley, bay leaf and thyme and cook for about 20 minutes, until the barley is tender to the bite. Stir in the kale, season with salt and pepper to taste and simmer for another 5 minutes, until the kale has wilted. If the soup feels quite thick, just add a little water to loosen. Serve hot with the soda bread for tearing and dunking (there's no need to remove the whole herbs, but you can do so, if you prefer).

# GLAZED CELERIAC STEAKS
## WITH A CHEESY CRUMB

1 celeriac (celery root), peeled
40g/1½oz/3 tablespoons butter,
    softened, plus extra for the chard
2 tablespoons wholegrain mustard
2 rosemary sprigs, leaves picked
    and chopped
100ml/3½fl oz/generous ⅓ cup
    dry white wine
100ml/3½fl oz/generous ⅓ cup
    vegetable stock
100ml/3½fl oz/generous ⅓ cup
    double (heavy) cream
2 tablespoons capers
200g/7oz rainbow chard, leaves and
    stalks separated, stalks chopped
salt and ground black pepper

### FOR THE CRUMB

small knob of butter
1 tablespoon olive oil
50g/1¾oz/1 cup panko breadcrumbs
25g/1oz Parmesan, grated
a small handful of flat-leaf parsley,
    leaves picked and chopped

SERVES | TOTAL TIME TO MAKE
4 | 00 HOURS | 30 MINS

**Although meat was a staple on the table during the early part of the 20th century, this recipe substitutes more typical beef steaks with thick slices of celeriac – without any compromise on flavour.**

Preheat your oven to 190°C/170°C fan/375°F/Gas 5 and line a roasting tin with baking paper. Place a griddle pan over a medium heat – but don't let it get too hot or it will burn the steaks.

Trim off the curved sides of the celeriac to give a flat surface all round. Cut 4 chunky slices, each about 2cm/¾in thick.

In a small bowl, mix together the butter with the mustard and rosemary with a generous seasoning of salt and pepper. Brush some of the flavoured butter on one side of each celeriac steak. Place the steaks, buttered side down, on the hot griddle. Cook for about 5 minutes, until you have nice, charred markings. Brush the uppermost side of each steak with more flavoured butter and turn the steaks over to char the other side.

While the steaks are cooking, make the crumb. Melt the butter in a frying pan with the olive oil, over a low–medium heat. Add the breadcrumbs and gently fry for 3–4 minutes, stirring, until golden. Remove from the heat, stir in the Parmesan and parsley, mix well and season with a little pepper. Set aside.

Transfer the charred steaks to the lined roasting tin. Brush over any remaining flavoured butter, and drizzle over the wine, vegetable stock and cream, then scatter over the capers. Spoon the crumb equally over the steaks and transfer everything to the oven to roast for 10 minutes, until the celeriac is tender but not too soft – you want a little bit of bite.

Meanwhile, melt a little butter in a medium saucepan over a medium heat. Add the chard stalks and cook for 3–4 minutes, until softened a little. Add the leaves with a splash of water, cover with a lid and cook for 2 minutes to wilt. Season with salt and pepper. Divide the chard between your plates, place a celeriac steak on each and spoon over any excess juices. Serve immediately.

# STEAK & ALE PIE WITH MASH

SERVES **4** | TOTAL TIME TO MAKE **02** HOURS **15** MINS

## FOR THE PASTRY

250g/9oz/1¾ cups strong
    white bread flour
½ teaspoon salt
60g/2¼oz/¼ cup butter,
    cubed and chilled
40g/1½oz/3 tablespoons lard, cubed
1 thyme sprig, leaves picked
1 teaspoon wholegrain mustard
40ml/1¼fl oz/2¾ tablespoons
    ice-cold water
1 egg, beaten

## FOR THE FILLING

3 tablespoons plain (all-purpose) flour
600g/1lb 5oz beef skirt, or chuck or
    braising steak, cut into 2cm/¾in dice
5 tablespoons vegetable oil
1 onion, roughly chopped
2 carrots, peeled and sliced
2 garlic cloves, finely chopped
6 chestnut mushrooms,
    roughly chopped
1 tablespoon tomato purée (paste)
500ml/17fl oz/generous 2 cups dark ale
2 tablespoons Worcestershire sauce
2 bay leaves
2 rosemary sprigs
salt and ground black pepper

## FOR THE MASH

500g/1lb 2oz all-rounder potatoes,
    peeled and cut into 5cm/2in pieces
50g/1¾oz/3½ tablespoons butter
100ml/3½fl oz/generous ⅓ cup
    full-fat milk
2 spring onions (scallions),
    finely chopped
75g/2½oz extra-mature
    Cheddar, crumbled
a few chives, finely chopped

You will need a 20–25cm/8–10in
pie dish (any shape will do).

We like to think that the weekly suppers at Watery Lane would have always included a hearty beef pie of some sort. For extra authenticity, you could add four or five shucked oysters to the stew.

Make the pastry. Tip the flour, salt, butter and lard into a bowl and rub them together until the mixture resembles breadcrumbs. Stir in the thyme and mustard, pour in the iced water and bring the dough together. Knead for 4–5 minutes, then wrap the dough in cling film and refrigerate while you make the filling.

Tip the flour into a large bowl and season with salt and pepper. Add the beef and toss to coat in the flour.

Heat 2 tablespoons of the vegetable oil in a large casserole over a high heat. Add the beef and fry it in batches until browned all over. Remove from the pan. Heat the remaining vegetable oil in the pan and cook the onion and carrots, keeping them moving, for about 5 minutes, until lightly browned. Add the garlic, mushrooms and tomato purée and fry for 3–4 minutes, until everything has a good colour. Add the ale, bring the liquid to the boil and add the Worcestershire sauce, bay leaves and rosemary. Reduce the heat, put the lid on the pan and simmer for about 1 hour, or until the beef is tender but not falling apart. Season with salt and pepper, then cool the filling completely (about 1 hour).

When you're ready to make the pie, preheat your oven to 180°C/160°C fan/350°F/Gas 4. Place the cold pie filling into your pie dish. Flour your work surface and roll out the pastry to about 3mm/⅛in thick and just larger than your pie dish. Cut some thin strips from the edge of the pastry and use some beaten egg to stick these around the rim of the dish. Brush the strips with egg.

Carefully place the pastry over the pie and press and crimp the edges to seal. Brush the pie lid all over with the remaining beaten egg, cut a couple of steam holes in the lid, and bake for about 40 minutes, until the pastry is golden and the filling is bubbling hot.

While the pie is baking, make the mash. Boil the potatoes in salted water for about 20–25 minutes, until tender. Drain them in a colander and leave them for 5 minutes to steam dry. Add the butter, milk and spring onions to the potato pan and tip the potatoes back in. Mash until smooth, then season. Spoon the mash into a serving dish and scatter over the cheese and chives. Serve the mash alongside the pie.

# ROAST RABBIT WITH BACON & MUSHROOMS IN A WHISKEY SAUCE

4 tablespoons vegetable oil
200g/7oz unsmoked streaky
    bacon, chopped
200g/7oz shallots, halved
1 carrot, peeled and thinly sliced
1 turnip (rutabaga), peeled and roughly
    chopped into 2–3cm/¾–1¼in pieces
150g/5½oz chestnut mushrooms,
    chopped or sliced
3½ tablespoons Irish whiskey
200ml/7fl oz/generous ¾ cup dry cider
300ml/10½fl oz/1¼ cups chicken stock
2 thyme sprigs
2 bay leaves
3 tablespoons plain (all-purpose) flour
450g/1lb skinless, boneless rabbit,
    diced into 3–4cm/1¼–1½in pieces
100ml/3½fl oz/generous ⅓ cup
    double (heavy) cream
1 tablespoon wholegrain mustard
a handful of flat-leaf parsley,
    leaves picked and chopped
salt and ground black pepper
steamed cabbage and boiled new
    potatoes, to serve

If you can't get hold of rabbit, use
the equivalent in chicken instead.

**Known in the 1920s as poor-man's chicken, rabbit was available to anyone who could hunt it down. And if you want to take Polly's advice, remember that 'Bucks taste better.'**

Heat 1 tablespoon of the vegetable oil in a large casserole over a medium heat. Add the bacon and cook for 5 minutes, until it's starting to crisp. Add the shallots, carrot and turnip and cook for 5–7 minutes, until the vegetables are getting a good colour. Add the mushrooms and fry for a couple more minutes, then pour in the whiskey and cider. Bring the liquid to a gentle boil and leave it to bubble away until reduced by about half (about 10 minutes). Add the stock, thyme and bay leaves, reduce the heat and simmer while you prepare the remaining ingredients.

Tip the flour into a large bowl and season with some salt and pepper. Add the rabbit and toss it around to coat, then shake off the excess flour and set aside.

Heat the remaining vegetable oil in a large frying pan over a medium heat. Add the rabbit pieces and cook, turning, for about 10 minutes, until browned all over.

Add the browned rabbit to the casserole, place a lid on the pan and leave to simmer over a low heat for about 1 hour, until the rabbit is tender. Stir the stew every so often so that it doesn't catch on the bottom of the pan. If the stew looks like it's getting too thick at any point, add a splash of water to loosen. Once it's ready, stir in the cream, mustard and parsley, season to taste and serve with steamed cabbage and boiled new potatoes.

SERVES | TOTAL TIME TO MAKE
4 | 01 HOUR | 50 MINS

# TOAD IN THE HOLE

8 good-quality pork sausages
8 rashers of smoked streaky bacon
1 large red onion, thickly sliced
2 tablespoons vegetable oil
2 rosemary sprigs, leaves picked
steamed greens (peas and runner
    beans would be good), to serve

### FOR THE BATTER

175g/6oz/1⅓ cups plain
    (all-purpose) flour
1 teaspoon salt
3 eggs
250ml/9fl oz/generous 1 cup
    full-fat milk
8 sage leaves, roughly chopped

### FOR THE GRAVY

20g/¾oz/1½ tablespoons butter
1 small onion, sliced
1 teaspoon light brown soft sugar
1 tablespoon balsamic vinegar
1 tablespoon plain (all-purpose) flour
300ml/10½fl oz/1¼ cups chicken stock
3 thyme sprigs, leaves picked
salt and ground black pepper

You will need an oven
dish, measuring roughly
25 x 20cm/10 x 8in.

SERVES **4** | TOTAL TIME TO MAKE **01** HOUR **10** MINS

**Zero-waste food for a thrifty family table, meat cooked in batter was the perfect way to make small quantities of expensive ingredients go further (and to use up any meat leftover from other meals, if there was any). In this recipe, the toads are given a twist – wrapped in bacon. Herby, rich gravy is a must.**

Preheat your oven to 200°C/180°C fan/400°F/Gas 6.

To make the batter, simply mix all the batter ingredients together in a bowl until smooth. Leave the batter somewhere warm.

Wrap each sausage in a rasher of streaky bacon. Place the wrapped sausages into the oven dish with the red onion, sprinkle in the vegetable oil and toss everything together. Bake for about 15–20 minutes, until the bacon starts to crisp.

Pour the batter into the dish, scatter over the rosemary leaves and bake for a further 30–35 minutes (without opening the oven door for at least the first 25 minutes), until the batter is puffed-up, crisp and golden.

While the toad in the hole is baking, make the gravy. Melt the butter in a small saucepan over a gentle heat. Add the onion and fry for about 7–10 minutes, until softened. Add the sugar and cook for a further 2–3 minutes, until the onion starts to brown. Pour in the vinegar and cook for 1 minute, then stir in the flour. Pour in the chicken stock, stir, and add the thyme leaves. Simmer the gravy for 15 minutes, until it is thickened and glossy. Season with salt and pepper, to taste. Turn off the heat and set the gravy aside to keep warm until the toad in the hole is ready. Serve together with buttered steamed greens on the side.

# SLOW-COOKED PIG'S FRY

200g/7oz chorizo, chopped into
  1cm/½in cubes
150g/5½oz smoked bacon lardons
2 rosemary sprigs, leaves picked
  and chopped
1 thyme sprig, leaves picked
butter, for greasing
1kg/2lb 4oz all-rounder potatoes,
  peeled and thinly sliced
1 swede (rutabaga), peeled
  and thinly sliced
2 large onions, thinly sliced
4 flat-leaf parsley sprigs, leaves
  and stalks roughly chopped
500ml/17fl oz/generous 2 cups
  beef or chicken stock
salt and ground black pepper
Alfie Solomons' Soda Bread
  (see page 12), thickly sliced
  and buttered, to serve

SERVES | TOTAL TIME TO MAKE
6 | 01 HOUR | 15 MINS

**Traditionally made with layers of potato, onion and tripe (or other offal), pig's fry is simple, satisfying food with loads of flavour. We've swapped out the tripe for bacon lardons and chorizo, but the Shelby family would definitely have been eating this the traditional way. Feel free to try it with tripe, if that takes your fancy – just soak the tripe in milk for 30 minutes, then drain and fry it like the bacon.**

Preheat your oven to 190°C/170°C fan/375°F/Gas 5.

Place a large frying pan over a medium heat. Add the chorizo and bacon lardons and fry for about 10 minutes, until the chorizo releases its oil and the bacon lardons are crisp. Remove the pan from the heat, stir in the rosemary and thyme and leave to cool.

Grease a roasting tin or oven dish with a little butter, then line it with a layer of sliced potato. Using one quarter of each, top with a layer of swede, a scattering of onions, a sprinkling of parsley and the chorizo and bacon mixture. Repeat the layering until you've used everything up, finishing with a layer of potato.

Warm the stock in a saucepan, season it with salt and pepper and pour it over the layers in the tray. Cover the tray tightly with foil, then place it in the oven and bake the pig's fry for 30 minutes. Then, remove the foil and bake it for a further 15 minutes, until the layers are tender and cooked through and the topping is golden and crisp – little burnt bits are a good thing and add to the flavour. Serve with some of Alfie's soda bread, thickly buttered, on the side.

# BAKED TROUT WITH RICE, FENNEL & LEMON

2 skin-on, filleted whole rainbow
  trout (each about 250g/9oz),
  washed and patted dry with
  kitchen paper
30g/1oz/¼ cup cooked white rice
finely grated zest of 1 small lemon
1 small fennel bulb, cored and
  finely chopped
50g/1¾oz/generous ⅓ cup
  frozen peas
a handful of flat-leaf parsley,
  leaves picked and chopped
5–6 dill fronds, chopped
100ml/3½fl oz/generous ⅓ cup
  dry white wine
a knob of butter, softened
salt and ground black pepper
steamed greens (such as samphire
  or green beans) and lemon
  wedges, to serve

When gangs go fishing, it might not mean quite the same thing as casting a rod for trout. Oysters, herring, mussels, cockles, sprats and eel were the catch most working-class families would have been eating in the early 20<sup>th</sup> century, but if you had your eyes set on social climbing, serving up trout would definitely have made a statement.

Preheat your oven to 190°C/170°C fan/375°F/Gas 5 and line a shallow roasting tin with baking paper. Find some kitchen string.

Place one half of each fish fillet, skin side down, on the lined roasting tin and season each with salt and pepper.

Tip the rice into a small mixing bowl and add the lemon zest, fennel, peas and both herbs. Season with salt and pepper and mix well. Divide the rice mixture between the two fillet halves, gently pressing it over the surface of the fish to coat. Place the second half of each fillet on top of the first, sandwiching the rice mixture in between. Tie your string around the fillets to secure them together, then pour the wine around the fish.

Brush the fish with the softened butter, season with salt and pepper and bake for 15 minutes, until the fish is cooked through. Serve with steamed greens, and with lemon wedges for squeezing over.

SERVES | TOTAL TIME TO MAKE
2 | 00 HOURS | 30 MINS

# LAMB & ROOT VEGETABLE STEW WITH DUMPLINGS

50g/1¾oz/generous ⅓ cup
   plain (all-purpose) flour
750g/1lb 10oz lamb shoulder,
   leg or neck end, cut into
   2.5cm/1in chunks
4 tablespoons vegetable oil
1 large onion, roughly chopped
2 salted anchovy fillets
2 carrots, peeled and cut into
   2cm/¾in slices
1 swede, peeled and roughly
   chopped into chunks
2 rosemary sprigs
2 bay leaves
200ml/7fl oz/generous ¾ cup
   dry white wine
750ml/26fl oz/3¼ cups lamb,
   chicken or vegetable stock
2 tablespoons Worcestershire sauce
salt and ground black pepper
a handful of flat-leaf parsley, leaves
   picked and chopped, to serve
steamed greens, to serve

## FOR THE DUMPLINGS

100g/3½oz/scant 1 cup
   (shredded) suet
200g/7oz/1½ cups self-raising flour
2 teaspoons wholegrain mustard
2 rosemary sprigs, leaves picked
   and chopped

**A bit of mutton dressed as lamb in this hearty stew. These days lamb is readily available, but a more authentic version would use mutton, so feel free to ask your local butcher for that instead, if you like. Alternatively, in the spirit of nothing-wasted, leftover roast lamb roughly chopped, would work a treat.**

Preheat your oven to 170°C/150°C fan/325°F/Gas 3.

Tip half of the flour into a large bowl and season with salt and pepper. Add the lamb and toss to coat in the flour. Heat 2 tablespoons of the oil in a large casserole over a high heat. Add half the lamb and fry until browned all over. Remove from the pan. Repeat with the remaining oil and lamb. Set aside on a plate.

Reduce the heat under the pan and add the onion and anchovies. Fry for 5–7 minutes, until the onion starts to brown. Return the lamb to the pan, and add the carrots, swede, rosemary, bay leaves and remaining flour, and then the white wine. Cook for 1–2 minutes, then pour in the stock and Worcestershire sauce. Season with salt and pepper, cover with a lid and pop the stew into the oven to cook for 1¼ hours, stirring once or twice during that time, until the lamb is tender.

Meanwhile, make the dumplings. Simply combine all the dumpling ingredients in a bowl, season with salt and pepper, and add 3–4 tablespoons of water, mixing to form a dough. Bring the dough together, then divide it into 12 equal pieces, rolling each piece into a ball. Set aside until the stew is ready.

Remove the cooked stew from the oven and nestle the dumplings into the sauce. Return the stew to the oven for 15 minutes, until the dumplings are plump and golden. Serve sprinkled with parsley, and some buttered steamed greens on the side.

SERVES **6** | TOTAL TIME TO MAKE **02** HOURS **00** MINS

# CREAMY BAKED RICE PUDDING WITH BERRY COMPÔTE

600ml/21fl oz/2½ cups semi-skimmed (reduced-fat) milk
200ml/7fl oz/generous ¾ cup double (heavy) cream
1 teaspoon vanilla extract
2 tablespoons caster (superfine) sugar
100g/3½oz/generous ½ cup pudding rice
1 bay leaf
¼ teaspoon freshly grated nutmeg

### FOR THE BERRY COMPÔTE

300g/10½oz frozen mixed berries
juice of 1 lemon
2 tablespoons light brown soft sugar

You will need a 1 litre/35fl oz oven dish, lightly greased with butter.

Warming, filling and comforting, rice pudding first became popular during the early 1900s. A spoonful of sweet jam made from foraged wild berries cuts through the creaminess. We've included a compôte here, but you can use a good-quality shop-bought jam, if you prefer.

Preheat your oven to 150°C/130°C fan/300°F/Gas 2.

Pour the milk and cream into a medium saucepan and add the vanilla and sugar. Place the pan over a medium–low heat and warm the mixture through for about 8–10 minutes. Meanwhile, tip the rice into the buttered oven dish.

Pour the warmed milk mixture into the oven dish and nestle in the bay leaf. Sprinkle over the grated nutmeg and bake for 1½ hours, until the rice is tender and you have a lovely brown skin on top.

While the rice pudding is baking, make the compôte. Tip all the compôte ingredients into a medium saucepan and place it over a high heat. Bring the juices to the boil, then reduce the heat and simmer for 20 minutes, until thickened and jammy. Leave to cool.

Serve the rice pudding hot in bowls with a generous spoonful of the compôte on top. (There's no need to remove the bay leaf.)

SERVES | TOTAL TIME TO MAKE
6 | 01 HOUR | 45 MINS

# MARMALADE BREAD & BUTTER PUDDING WITH RUM CUSTARD

9 slices of slightly stale white
　　bread, crusts removed
120g/4¼oz/generous ½ cup
　　butter, softened
about 225g/8oz orange marmalade
50g/1¾oz/⅓ cup sultanas
　　(golden raisins)
3 large egg yolks
100g/3½oz/½ cup caster
　　(superfine) sugar
1 tablespoon vanilla extract
a little grated nutmeg
600ml/21fl oz/2½ cups full-fat milk

### FOR THE CUSTARD

350ml/12fl oz/1½ cups full-fat milk
1½–2 tablespoons dark rum
1 teaspoon vanilla extract
3 egg yolks
2 tablespoons caster (superfine) sugar
1 teaspoon cornflour (cornstarch)

You will need a 2 litre/70fl oz oven
dish, lightly greased with butter.

SERVES **6** — TOTAL TIME TO MAKE **01** HOUR | **00** MINS

**Stale bread reinvents beautifully into this traditional family dessert. The longer you leave the pudding to soak before baking it, the better your results. Once again, the spirit of Alfie Solomons inspires this dish with the rum-laced custard.**

Take 3 slices of bread. Spread one side of each slice with butter and marmalade. Cut the slices in half diagonally and arrange them in the dish, slightly overlapping. Sprinkle over half the sultanas. Repeat with another 3 slices and the remaining sultanas, then repeat for the final 3 slices of bread (without sultanas this time).

In a large jug, whisk together the egg yolks, sugar, vanilla, nutmeg and milk. Pour the mixture all over the bread in the dish, gently pressing down with your fingers so that all the bread absorbs the milky mixture. Leave the dish in the fridge for about 30 minutes, or longer if you have time. Preheat your oven to 170°C/150°C fan/325°F/Gas 3.

Remove the soaked pudding from the fridge and bake it for 45–50 minutes, until well risen and spongy to the touch.

While the pudding is baking, get on with the custard. Place the milk, rum and vanilla into a saucepan and warm the mixture over a gentle heat, until lukewarm. In a mixing bowl, beat together the egg yolks, sugar and cornflour with a wooden spoon.

Stirring continuously, slowly pour the warm milk on to the egg mixture in the bowl. Pour the combined mixture back into the milk pan and place it over a low heat. Stir gently until thickened so that it leaves a distinct line if you run your finger through it over the back of a spoon. Don't stop stirring until you reach this point, otherwise the custard may scramble. Keep warm until you're ready to serve it with the hot bread and butter pudding.

# AT THE BAR OF THE GARRISON

# CRISPY WHITEBAIT
## WITH TARTARE SAUCE

vegetable oil, for deep-frying
25g/1oz/¼ cup cornflour (cornstarch)
3 tablespoons plain (all-purpose) flour
½ teaspoon cayenne pepper,
    plus optional extra for sprinkling
¼ teaspoon ground black pepper
½ teaspoon salt
1 egg, beaten
400g/14oz fresh or thawed
    frozen whitebait
flaky (kosher) sea salt, for sprinkling

**FOR THE TARTARE SAUCE**

3 tablespoons mayonnaise
3 cornichons, finely chopped
1 tablespoon capers, finely chopped
a small handful of flat-leaf parsley,
    leaves picked and finely chopped

**There's something deeply satisfying about crunching into a crispy whitebait with a pint of ale in tow. You can make your own mayonnaise if you like, but good-quality store-bought will make this a quick snack to pull together when you're feeling peckish.**

First, make the tartare sauce by spooning the mayonnaise into a small bowl and mixing through all the remaining ingredients. Set aside until you're ready to serve.

If you have a deep-fat fryer, heat the oil to 180°C/350°F. If not, one third fill a medium saucepan with vegetable oil and place it over a medium heat. The oil is ready when the temperature reaches 180°C/350°F on a digital cooking thermometer, or when a cube of bread floats and browns within 30 seconds.

Sift both flours, the cayenne pepper, black pepper and salt into a mixing bowl. Tip the beaten egg into another bowl. Add half the whitebait to the bowl with the egg, turning to coat, then toss them through the flour mixture, making sure all the fish are covered. Shake off the excess and deep-fry the fish for about 3–4 minutes, until crispy. Set the first half aside to drain on kitchen paper while you coat and deep-fry the second batch.

Serve the whitebait hot, sprinkled with flaky sea salt and extra cayenne pepper, if you like, and with the tartare sauce for dipping.

SERVES | TOTAL TIME TO MAKE

4 | 00 HOURS | 20 MINS

# SCOTCH EGGS WITH MUSTARD MAYONNAISE

SERVES **6** | TOTAL TIME TO MAKE **01** HOUR **00** MINS

6 large eggs
300g/10½oz good-quality
   pork sausages
5 sage leaves, finely chopped
a small handful of flat-leaf parsley,
   leaves picked and chopped
½ teaspoon ground black pepper
50g/1¾oz/generous ⅓ cup plain
   (all-purpose) flour
1 egg, beaten with 2 tablespoons
   full-fat milk
150g/5½oz/3 cups panko
   breadcrumbs
vegetable oil, for deep-frying
a handful of watercress,
   to serve (optional)

### FOR THE DIP

4 tablespoons mayonnaise
1 tablespoon English mustard
¼ bunch of chives, chopped
salt and ground black pepper

**Tommy might insist on Fabergé Eggs, but we think these Scotch eggs at the bar of The Garrison will cause far less trouble! Make sure you get your oil good and hot to guarantee a crispy outer crumb.**

Bring a large pan of water to the boil and carefully lower in the eggs. Boil them for 6 minutes to soft set the yolks, then remove them with a slotted spoon and place them in a bowl of iced water. Once the eggs are cold, peel them and set them aside.

Squeeze the sausage meat from the sausage skins into a mixing bowl. Add the sage, parsley and black pepper and mix well.

Divide the sausage mixture into 6 equal-sized balls. Place one of the balls on a piece of baking paper, and flatten it with a damp hand. Place an egg in the middle of the sausage-meat disc and bring the meat up and around the egg. Gently press the sausage meat around the egg, making sure that the egg is wrapped. Repeat with the remaining balls of sausage meat and eggs.

Tip the flour into one wide, shallow bowl, the beaten egg into another and the breadcrumbs into a third. One by one, roll the coated eggs in the flour, making sure they are well covered. Then, turn them in the beaten egg, lifting them out with a fork, and finally turn them in the breadcrumbs to coat – make sure the whole egg is covered in the crumb. Just before frying, preheat your oven to 150°C/130°C fan/300°F/Gas 2.

If you have a deep-fat fryer, heat the oil to 180°C/350°F. If not, one third fill a medium saucepan with vegetable oil and place it over a medium heat. The oil is ready when the temperature reaches 180°C/350°F on a digital cooking thermometer, or when a cube of bread floats and browns within 30 seconds. Deep-fry the Scotch eggs in batches of 1–3 eggs at a time, depending on the size of your pan and taking care not to overfill, for about 5–7 minutes per batch, turning occasionally, until golden and crispy all over. Remove the cooked eggs to a plate lined with kitchen paper and keep warm in the oven while you deep-fry the remainder.

To make the dip, mix the mayonnaise with the mustard and chives and season with salt and pepper to taste. Serve the warm Scotch eggs with the dip, and a watercress salad, if you wish.

# PORK SCRATCHING STICKS WITH SMOKED PAPRIKA & SEA SALT

1 piece of pork skin (about
    400–500g/14oz–1lb 2oz)
salt, for sprinkling
boiling water from a kettle
½ teaspoon smoked paprika
1 teaspoon flaky (kosher) sea salt

**This snack is so moreish — something to get your teeth into while you plot your next move. Ask your butcher for pork skin — it should be fairly cheap and easy to get hold of.**

Preheat your oven to 220°C/200°C fan/425°F/Gas 7.

Place the pork skin on a baking tray and, using a kitchen blow torch, singe off any hairs. Sprinkle the skin liberally with fine salt and leave the skin for 20 minutes – the salt will draw out the moisture. Then, put the pork skin into a clean sink and pour over the boiling water. Dry the skin completely with kitchen paper.

Line a baking tray with baking paper and pop the dry skin on to it. Using a pair of sharp kitchen scissors, cut the skin into 1–2cm/½–¾in strips or bitesize pieces (or a mixture). Place another piece of baking paper on top of the strips or pieces and put another heavy baking tray on top of that. Transfer the baking trays, with the pork skin sandwiched between them, to the oven and bake for 30 minutes. Check to see if the skin is crisping. If not, pop the skin back into the oven without the uppermost tray and bake it for a further 10 minutes, or until crispy.

Remove the pork scratchings from the oven and transfer them to a plate lined with kitchen paper to drain. Tip them into a bowl and sprinkle over the smoked paprika and flaky sea salt. Toss to coat, then, once the scratchings have cooled, transfer them to an airtight container to store – they'll keep like this for a week.

| SERVES | TOTAL TIME TO MAKE | |
|---|---|---|
| 4 | 00 HOURS | 55 MINS |

# GRILLED OYSTERS
## WITH PARMESAN CRUMB

12 oysters in their shells
3½ tablespoons double (heavy) cream
a knob of butter, melted
25g/1oz/½ cup panko breadcrumbs
10g/¼oz Parmesan, grated
a small handful of flat-leaf parsley,
    leaves picked and finely chopped
ground black pepper
flaky (kosher) sea salt, to serve

**Oysters were once served as a street snack and definitely the kind of thing you'd have with a whiskey at The Garrison. If you don't feel comfortable shucking your own oysters, you could ask your fishmonger to do it for you. Use them on the day you buy them and keep the juices for extra flavour.**

First, shuck your oysters. One at a time, place an oyster, flat side up, on a folded tea towel and lift the tea towel up over the oyster to protect your hand. Insert a shucking knife (or, if you don't have one, a table knife) into the hinge of the oyster. When you feel it go in, twist the knife and the shell should pop open. Run the knife across the inside of the upper part of the shell to release the oyster. Then run it under the oyster. Remove the oyster from the bottom shell, run the shell under water to rinse it, then place the oyster back in the shell. Place the opened shell into a grill pan, supporting it with scrunched-up foil to keep it upright while you shuck the remainder.

Preheat your grill to high. Spoon the cream over the oysters and season with a little pepper.

Combine the melted butter, breadcrumbs, Parmesan and parsley in a small bowl to make a crumb. Scatter the crumb over the oysters and then place them under the hot grill for 4–5 minutes, until the shellfish are cooked and the crumb is golden.

Serve the oysters straight away, supporting the oysters on a bed of flaky sea salt to keep them upright.

SERVES | TOTAL TIME TO MAKE
2 | 00 HOURS | 20 MINS

# MINI CURRIED LAMB PIES

1 tablespoon olive oil
1 small onion, finely chopped
2 garlic cloves, finely chopped
1 carrot, peeled and grated
250g/9oz lean lamb mince
1 tablespoon medium curry powder
50g/1¾oz frozen peas
1 teaspoon tomato purée (paste)
2 teaspoons mango chutney
100ml/3½fl oz/generous ⅓ cup
    lamb stock
1 x 500g/1lb 2oz block of
    shortcrust pastry
1 egg, lightly beaten
1 teaspoon black onion seeds
salt and ground black pepper

You will need a 6-cup muffin tin, lightly greased with butter; and 11cm/4¼in and 7–8cm/2¾–3¼in round pastry cutters (or equivalent).

MAKES 6 — TOTAL TIME TO MAKE 01 HOUR 10 MINS

**Spices, particularly curry spices, were becoming very popular in Britain during the early 20th century. These little pies would have felt very new and exotic served up at The Garrison bar.**

Preheat your oven to 200°C/180°C fan/400°F/Gas 6.

Heat the olive oil in a large saucepan over a low heat. Add the onion, garlic and carrot and fry for about 10 minutes, until soft but not coloured. Add the lamb mince and cook, stirring to break up the meat, until just browned. Stir in the curry powder and frozen peas and cook for 2–3 minutes, until the curry powder is fragrant. Spoon in the tomato purée and mango chutney. Season with salt and pepper, cook for a few more minutes, then stir in the lamb stock. Remove from the heat and leave to cool completely.

Roll out the pastry to a disk about 5mm/¼in thick. Using the 11cm/4¼in round pastry cutter, cut out 6 pastry disks and use them to line the cups in the muffin tin, pressing the pastry into the base of each hollow and leaving a slight overhang. Set the remaining pastry aside. Divide the cold filling between the pastry cases and brush the overhanging edges with the beaten egg.

Gather up the pastry trimmings and re-roll them to about 5mm/¼in thick. Use the 7–8cm/2¾–3¼in round pastry cutter to cut out 6 disks. Place 1 disk on top of each filled case to create a pie lid. Press around the edge to seal in the filling.

Brush the lids with the remaining beaten egg and make a small hole in the middle of each pie to let the steam escape. Scatter each pie with black onion seeds and bake the pies in the middle of the oven for 25–30 minutes, until golden. Serve warm.

# FRIED CHEESE & ALE SANDWICHES

a knob of butter
40g/1½oz/generous ¼ cup plain
    (all-purpose) flour
100ml/3½fl oz ale,
    at room temperature
100ml/3½fl oz/generous ⅓ cup
    full-fat milk
1 teaspoon English mustard
2 tablespoons Worcestershire sauce
100g/3½oz mature Cheddar, grated
¼ teaspoon ground black pepper
¼ bunch of chives, chopped
4 slices of crusty white bloomer
a handful of spinach leaves
2 eggs, beaten
vegetable oil, for frying
gherkins, to serve

| MAKES | TOTAL TIME TO MAKE | |
| --- | --- | --- |
| 2 | 00 HOURS | 50 MINS |

**By the early 20th century, the sandwich had been around for years. The toastie, on the other hand, was just gaining popularity – this one is a chunky, full-on, heavyweight fried cheese sandwich.**

Melt the butter in a small saucepan over a low heat. Add the flour and cook for 1 minute, stirring continuously. Keep stirring and slowly add the ale. Once the ale is fully incorporated, add the milk, mustard and Worcestershire sauce and stir to combine to a smooth, thick sauce. Add the Cheddar, black pepper and chives, stirring to melt the cheese into the sauce. Once melted, remove the pan from the heat and leave the sauce to cool. It will be quite thick, but that's what you're after.

Generously spread two slices of the bread with the cheese sauce, add a layer of spinach leaves to one slice and place the second slice, cheese sauce down, on top, gently pressing the sandwich together.

Heat a large, non-stick frying pan over a medium heat, and pour the beaten egg into a wide, shallow bowl.

Dip the sandwich into the egg, wait a few minutes, then turn it over and leave the other side to soak briefly in the egg, too.

Add a little vegetable oil to the frying pan and fry the sandwich for about 6–7 minutes, until golden on the underside. Carefully flip it over using a spatula and cook on the other side for a further 4–5 minutes, until that side is golden, too. Don't worry if some of the cheese sauce oozes out. Remove the sandwich from the pan, slice it in half and serve it straight away with a few gherkins on the side – and, of course, a glass of ale. Repeat for the remaining slices of bread and filling. Cheers!

# RAISED MINI PORK & HERB PIES

## FOR THE PASTRY

450g/1lb/scant 3½ cups plain
    (all-purpose) flour
1 teaspoon salt
80g/2¾oz/⅓ cup butter
80g/2¾oz/⅓ cup lard

## FOR THE FILLING

250g/9oz lean pork sausage meat
100g/3½oz pork loin, finely chopped
4 sage leaves, finely chopped
100g/3½oz unsmoked streaky
    bacon, finely chopped
½ teaspoon English mustard
1 egg, beaten
3 gelatine leaves
200ml/7fl oz/generous ¾ cup
    warm chicken stock
salt and ground black pepper
homemade or shop-bought
    apple chutney, to serve

You will need a 6-cup muffin tin,
lightly greased with butter; 11cm/4¼in
and 7–8cm/2¾–3¼in round pastry
cutters (or equivalent); and a small
icing nozzle.

MAKES 6 — TOTAL TIME TO MAKE 01 HOUR 20 MINS

We're keeping things simple for our pork pies and using a muffin tin to give them their tall sides. At The Garrison, though, the pastry would have been 'raised' by hand.

Preheat your oven to 180°C/160°C fan/350°F/Gas 4.

Make the pastry. Combine the flour and salt in a mixing bowl. Pour 200ml/7fl oz/generous ¾ cup of water into a medium saucepan and add the butter and lard. Place the pan over a medium heat and bring the liquid to the boil. Once the fats have melted, remove the pan from the heat. Pour the hot fats into the bowl with the flour and mix with a wooden spoon to form a dough. Cover with cling film and keep warm while you make the filling.

Place the sausage meat, pork loin, sage, bacon and mustard into a mixing bowl, season with salt and pepper and, using your hands, mix well.

Break off two thirds of the warm pastry (leave the remainder, covered, in the bowl) and roll it out on a lightly floured surface to a circle about 3mm/⅛in thick. Using the 11cm/4¼in round pastry cutter, cut out 6 disks and use them to line the cups in the muffin tin, pressing the pastry into the base of each hollow and leaving an overhang. Divide the pork mixture between the pastry cases and brush the rim of the pastry with beaten egg.

Roll out the remaining pastry to about 3mm/⅛in thick. Using the smaller round cutter, cut out 6 disks to form the pie lids. Place 1 disk over the pork filling in each hollow and press the edges together, crimping to seal and making sure there are no gaps. Make a small hole in the centre of each pie lid (this needs to be big enough for the end of a piping nozzle to squeeze in), then brush the lids with the beaten egg. Bake the pies for about 40 minutes, until the filling is cooked through and the pastry is golden. Remove the pies from the oven and leave to cool in the tin.

Meanwhile, soak the gelatine in cold water for 5 minutes, until soft. Remove the sheets from the water, squeeze out the excess and stir them into the warm stock in a jug. Leave to cool.

One pie at a time, insert the piping nozzle into the hole in the lid and use it as a funnel to pour a little of the stock into each pie. Leave the pies to go cold and the jelly to set, then remove the pies from the muffin tin and serve with apple chutney.

# SCOTCH WOODCOCK

2 thick slices of seeded
   granary bread
a knob of butter, softened
2 teaspoons gentleman's
   relish or anchovy paste
3½ tablespoons double
   (heavy) cream
3 eggs, beaten
4 salted anchovy fillets
1 teaspoon capers
¼ bunch of chives, chopped
½ punnet of mustard cress, sliced
salt and ground black pepper

**The Scots' answer to Welsh Rarebit (rabbit), Scotch woodcock doesn't contain any woodcock at all – rather, it is scrambled eggs and anchovies on toast. It's thought to have first been served during Victorian times.**

Toast or griddle the slices of bread, making sure you have good colour on them. Spread one side of each slice with a little of the butter, leaving enough butter to use for the scrambled eggs, then spread each slice with half of the gentleman's relish.

Melt the remaining butter in a non-stick frying pan over a low heat and add the cream. Warm through, then add the beaten eggs, seasoning with salt and pepper to taste (remember that the anchovies are salted, so you won't need much salt). Slowly cook the eggs, stirring, until they form a fairly loose, wet scramble.

Pile the scrambled eggs on to the slices of toast, top with equal amounts of the anchovies and capers, and scatter with the chives and mustard cress. Serve straight away.

| SERVES | TOTAL TIME TO MAKE | |
|---|---|---|
| 2 | 00 HOURS | 20 MINS |

# APPLE FRITTERS
## WITH CINNAMON SUGAR

### FOR THE BATTER

100g/3½oz/¾ cup plain
(all-purpose) flour
50g/1¾oz/½ cup cornflour
(corn starch)
3 tablespoons icing
(confectioners') sugar
a pinch of salt
1 teaspoon baking powder
1 egg
1 teaspoon vanilla extract
½ teaspoon ground cinnamon
200ml/7fl oz/generous ¾ cup
sparkling water
vegetable oil, for deep-frying

### FOR THE APPLES

2–3 firm eating apples (such as
Cox, Granny Smith or Braeburn),
peeled, cored and sliced into
5mm/¼in rings
juice of ½ lemon
100g/3½oz/½ cup caster
(superfine) sugar
½ teaspoon ground cinnamon
dollops of whipped cream,
to serve (optional)

**Sold as street snacks perhaps to soak up some of the whiskey for those on the way out of the pub more than in it, these fritters are a great way to use up apples that are past their best.**

Make the batter. Sift both flours, and the icing sugar, salt and baking powder into a large mixing bowl. Crack in the egg and add the vanilla, cinnamon and sparkling water. Whisk until smooth and set aside.

If you have a deep-fat fryer, heat the oil to 190°C/375°F. If not, one third fill a medium saucepan with vegetable oil and place it over a medium heat. The oil is ready when the temperature reaches 190°C/375°F on a digital cooking thermometer, or when a cube of bread floats and browns within 25–30 seconds.

Meanwhile, prepare the apples by tossing them in a bowl with the lemon juice to stop them browning.

In batches of about 4 rings at a time, using a fork, dip the apple rings into the rested batter, then lift them out and pop them straight into the hot oil. Deep-fry for about 4 minutes, turning halfway through, until the fritters are golden and crisp all over. Remove the fritters from the oil and set them aside to drain on kitchen paper while you deep-fry the remainder.

Meanwhile, mix the caster sugar and cinnamon together in a wide, shallow bowl or baking tray. Tip in the warm apple fritters and toss them in the spiced sugar to coat. Serve the fritters just as they are, or with an indulgent dollop of whipped cream for dipping, if you like.

SERVES | TOTAL TIME TO MAKE
6 | 00 HOURS | 30 MINS

# LUNCH AT THE DERBY

# POTTED SHRIMPS
## WITH PICKLED CUCUMBER

250g/9oz/generous 1 cup butter
3 shallots, finely chopped
1 garlic clove, chopped
¼ teaspoon freshly grated nutmeg
finely grated zest of ½ lemon
250g/9oz cooked and peeled
    brown shrimps
¼ teaspoon cayenne pepper
4 small bay leaves
salt and ground black pepper
4 slices of granary bread, toasted
    (and buttered, if you wish),
    to serve

### FOR THE PICKLED CUCUMBER

½ cucumber, thinly sliced
½ teaspoon salt
1 tablespoon caster (superfine) sugar
1 tablespoon white wine vinegar
1 teaspoon yellow mustard seeds
5 dill fronds, leaves picked
    and chopped

You will need 4 ramekins.

| SERVES | TOTAL TIME TO MAKE | |
| --- | --- | --- |
| 4 | 00 HOURS | 30 MINS |

**We have been harvesting brown shrimps for hundreds of years. The traditional way to prepare them would be to boil them in sea water to maintain their sweetness, toss them with butter and spices, then pot them in a jar and seal with clarified butter. They make a sophisticated light lunch for someone trying to move up in the world.**

Put the butter in a small saucepan over a very low heat with the shallots, garlic and nutmeg. Once the butter has melted, remove the pan from the heat and add the lemon zest. Leave the butter to infuse for 5 minutes.

In a bowl, toss the shrimps with the cayenne pepper and season with salt and pepper. Divide the shrimps equally between your 4 ramekins.

Strain the butter through a fine sieve into a jug. Discard the contents of the sieve. Pour equal amounts of the butter over the shrimps in the ramekins, making sure the shrimps are completely covered. Pop a bay leaf on top of each serving and transfer the ramekins to the fridge to set (about 30 minutes).

While the potted shrimps are setting, make the pickled cucumber. Place the cucumber slices into a sieve, sprinkle over the salt and leave them over a bowl for 10 minutes while the cucumber slices release their liquid.

In a separate small bowl, mix together the sugar, vinegar and mustard seeds. Squeeze the cucumber slices to release any excess water and add the slices to the vinegar mixture, along with the chopped dill. Toss everything together.

Serve the potted shrimps with the pickled cucumber and toasted granary bread on the side.

# ANGELS ON HORSEBACK

12 shucked oysters
(see page 50 for shucking
instructions, if needed)
6 rashers of smoked streaky
bacon, cut in half
1 tablespoon maple syrup
1 tablespoon wholegrain mustard
1 lemon, cut into 4 wedges
a small handful of flat-leaf parsley,
leaves picked and chopped

You will need 4 small wooden
or metal skewers.

If you're not in the mood for 'angels',
try devils on horseback instead –
use pitted prunes each stuffed with
a blanched almond or a little blue
cheese and then wrapped in bacon.

**Oysters would likely have been standard fare at a food stall at the races. Wrapped in bacon to become angels on horseback, they are a fitting morsel to whet the appetite before throwing good money at the bookie stands.**

Preheat your grill to medium. One at a time, place each oyster at the end of a piece of bacon and wrap the bacon around it. Thread 3 wrapped oysters on to each skewer and transfer the skewers to a grill pan. You'll end up with 4 skewers of 3 oysters each.

Combine the maple syrup and mustard in a small bowl to make a glaze and, using a pastry brush, brush the glaze all over the bacon wrapping. Thread a lemon wedge on to each skewer.

Grill the angels on horseback for 2 minutes, then turn them over and grill for a further 1 minute, until the bacon crisps up. Remove the skewers from the grill and sprinkle with the parsley.

Serve the oysters straight away with the lemon wedges for squeezing over.

SERVES 2 | TOTAL TIME TO MAKE 00 HOURS 15 MINS

# ENGLISH SUMMER SALAD

SERVES **4** | TOTAL TIME TO MAKE **00** HOURS | **40** MINS

400g/14oz new potatoes, halved
3 or 4 eggs
12 asparagus spears,
    woody ends removed
150g/5½oz green beans, halved
100g/3½oz podded broad beans
a handful of watercress
2 baby gem lettuces, quartered
2 tomatoes, chopped into chunks
6 radishes, thinly sliced
1 punnet of mustard cress, sliced
¼ bunch of chives, chopped
5–6 dill fronds, roughly chopped
3–4 mint sprigs, leaves picked
    and chopped
4–8 slices of Alfie Solomons' Soda
    Bread (see page 12), to serve

## FOR THE DRESSING

3 egg yolks
3 tablespoons malt vinegar
1 teaspoon caster (superfine) sugar
1 teaspoon English mustard
¼ teaspoon cayenne pepper
200ml/7fl oz/generous ¾ cup
    rapeseed oil (or any flavourless oil)
100ml/3½fl oz/generous ⅓ cup
    double (heavy) cream
salt and ground black pepper

**Asparagus season really comes into full swing in June, making this the perfect light lunch to enjoy from your box at the Epsom Derby.**

Boil the potatoes in a pan of salted water for about 20 minutes, until just tender, then drain them and leave them to cool completely (don't refresh them under cold water). In the same pan, while the potatoes are boiling, boil the eggs for 6½ minutes, then remove them from the pan and refresh them in a bowl of iced water. When they're cool enough to handle, peel them and set them aside until needed.

Make the dressing. Whisk together the egg yolks, vinegar, sugar, mustard and cayenne pepper in a medium bowl. Whisking continuously, slowly pour in the oil, in just a thin trickle, so that the dressing emulsifies and thickens. When it's thick, whisk in the cream and season with salt and pepper. Leave to one side.

Pour about 100ml/3½fl oz/generous ⅓ cup of water into a medium saucepan and bring it to the boil. Add the asparagus, green beans and broad beans and boil, with the lid on, for about 2–3 minutes, until just tender – you really want to keep a bite to the asparagus. Drain and leave to cool.

Arrange the watercress, baby gem, new potatoes, tomatoes, asparagus, green beans and broad beans over a serving platter. Scatter over the radishes and mustard cress. Halve the boiled eggs and arrange the halves over the salad. Drizzle over half the dressing, then finally, sprinkle over the herbs. Serve with the remaining dressing alongside for drizzling over, and with slices or hunks of soda bread.

# SANDWICH PLATTER

These sandwiches turn the notion of humble bread and filling into something far more fitting for the rising social classes. Each filling is enough to make two sandwiches for slicing into smaller fingers or triangles, if you like.

1 gammon steak, fat removed
2 tablespoons orange marmalade
4 tablespoons mayonnaise
juice of ½ lemon
1 teaspoon Dijon mustard
a small bunch of flat-leaf parsley,
    leaves picked and chopped
1 small red onion, finely sliced
1 carrot, coarsely grated
50g/1¾oz red or white cabbage,
    finely shredded
1 teaspoon English mustard
1 large gherkin, finely chopped
butter, for spreading
2 crusty bread or ciabatta rolls,
    sliced open
4 cos lettuce leaves
¼ bunch of chives, chopped
salt and ground black pepper

| MAKES | TOTAL TIME TO MAKE | |
|---|---|---|
| 2 | 00 HOURS | 25 MINS |

## POLLY'S MARMALADE-GLAZED HAM ROLL

Preheat your grill to medium. Brush the gammon steak with half the marmalade and grill it, brushed side up, for 3–4 minutes. Turn it over, brush it with the remaining marmalade and grill for another 3 minutes to cook through. Leave to cool.

Make a 'slaw. Combine 2 tablespoons of the mayo with the lemon juice, Dijon mustard and parsley and season with salt and pepper. Mix well. Stir in the onion, carrot and cabbage. Set aside.

In a small bowl, mix the remaining mayo with the English mustard, gherkin and a little black pepper.

To build the sandwich, butter the cut sides of the rolls, then spread the bottom half of each with some of the English mustard mayo. Top each with a couple of cos leaves and spoonfuls of the 'slaw. Slice the gammon and add the slices on top, then spoon on any remaining mustard mayo, or to taste. Sprinkle with the chives, top with the roll lids and serve.

3 tablespoons white wine vinegar
2 tablespoons caster (superfine) sugar
1 teaspoon yellow mustard seeds
1 red onion, sliced
a knob of butter
1 leek, cut into 1cm/½in slices
100g/3½oz Cheshire cheese (use a good
    Cheddar if you can't get Cheshire)
a small handful of watercress,
    roughly chopped
4 walnut halves, chopped
4 slices of seeded wholemeal
    (wholewheat) bread, lightly buttered
1 punnet of mustard cress, sliced

| MAKES | TOTAL TIME TO MAKE | |
|---|---|---|
| 2 | 00 HOURS | 20 MINS |

## CHESHIRE CHEESE, LEEK & WALNUT SANDWICH

Pour the vinegar, caster sugar, mustard seeds and 1 tablespoon of water into a small saucepan and place it over a low heat, warming the mixture until the sugar has dissolved. Remove from the heat, add the onion and set aside while you make the cheese filling.

Melt the butter in a small frying pan over a medium heat. Add the leek and a splash of water and fry for 2–3 minutes to soften a little. Set aside to cool. Once cooled, crumble in the cheese, and add the watercress and half the walnuts. Stir to combine.

Drain the onion, discarding the pickling liquid.

Pile the cheese mixture on to 2 of the buttered bread slices, top with the pickled red onion, sprinkle over the remaining walnuts and finish with the mustard cress. Sandwich with the remaining slices of buttered bread and cut into fingers, if you wish.

3 eggs
2 rashers of unsmoked streaky bacon
2 tablespoons mayonnaise
1 teaspoon English mustard
¼ teaspoon cayenne pepper
1 teaspoon white wine vinegar
a handful of watercress
2–4 slices of sourdough bread,
    lightly buttered
1 teaspoon capers
¼ bunch of chives, chopped
4 anchovy fillets, drained from a jar
salt and ground black pepper

MAKES 2 | TOTAL TIME TO MAKE 00 HOURS | 20 MINS

# DEVILLED EGGS WITH ANCHOVY, CAPERS & WATERCRESS SOURDOUGH

Bring a large pan of water to the boil over a high heat. Add the eggs and boil for 10 minutes to set the yolks. Remove the eggs using a slotted spoon and place in a bowl of iced water to cool. Once cooled, peel the eggs and set them aside.

While the eggs are boiling, place a non-stick frying pan over a medium–hot heat and add the bacon rashers. Fry for about 5 minutes on one side, then 3 minutes on the other, until crisp. Remove from the pan and leave to cool, then roughly chop.

Combine the mayonnaise, mustard, cayenne pepper and vinegar in a bowl. Add the eggs and, using a blunt knife, roughly chop them, folding them into the flavoured mayo as you go. Season with a little salt and pepper.

Scatter the watercress over two of the buttered bread slices. Divide the egg mixture equally over the top, then scatter over the bacon, capers and chives. Add the anchovies, then sandwich with the remaining two slices of buttered bread, or serve as an 'open' sandwich without the top slices, if you prefer.

3 tablespoons full-fat cream cheese
1 teaspoon horseradish sauce
5 dill fronds, leaves picked and chopped
finely grated zest of ½ lemon
2 slices of pumpernickel or rye bread
200g/7oz smoked salmon slices
1 punnet of mustard cress, sliced
salt and ground black pepper

### FOR THE PICKLES

4 tablespoons white wine vinegar
2 tablespoons caster (superfine) sugar
1 teaspoon yellow mustard seeds
4 radishes, quartered
¼ cucumber, peeled and thinly sliced
1 beetroot (beet), peeled and
    thinly sliced

MAKES 2 | TOTAL TIME TO MAKE 00 HOURS | 30 MINS

# OPEN SMOKED SALMON SANDWICH WITH PICKLES

First, make the pickles. Place the vinegar, sugar, mustard seeds and 3 tablespoons of water in a small saucepan over a low heat until the sugar has dissolved.

Place the radishes and cucumber into one small bowl and the beetroot into another. Pour the pickling liquor into each bowl to cover the vegetables, stir, and leave both bowls for about 20 minutes for the contents to lightly pickle, then drain.

Meanwhile, combine the cream cheese, horseradish sauce, dill and lemon zest in a bowl and season with salt and pepper.

Spread each slice of bread with the cream cheese mixture and top with equal amounts of the betroot and then the smoked salmon. Arrange the pickled radishes and cucumber over the top of the smoked salmon and finish with a scattering of mustard cress.

# APPLE CHARLOTTE

250g/9oz cooking apples
(such as Bramley), peeled,
cored and chopped into
2cm/¾in chunks
300g/10½oz eating apples
(such as Braeburn, Cox or
Pippin), peeled, cored and
chopped into 2cm/¾in chunks
1 tablespoon caster (superfine) sugar
¼ teaspoon ground cinnamon
finely grated zest and juice of 1 lemon
2 tablespoons calvados (optional)
7 slices of white bread,
crusts removed
100g/3½oz/scant ½ cup
butter, melted

### FOR THE SWEET CREAM

200ml/7fl oz/generous ¾ cup
double (heavy) cream
1 tablespoons icing
(confectioners') sugar
½ teaspoon vanilla extract

You will need a 1 litre/35fl oz
ovenproof pudding bowl.

SERVES **4** TOTAL TIME TO MAKE **01** HOUR **10** MINS

**We like the idea of this quintessential English pudding (created in the 19th century for King George IV) to finish a lunch at the races. You could make individual versions in ramekins, if you prefer.**

Place all the apple pieces into a medium saucepan with the caster sugar, cinnamon and lemon zest and juice. Cook over a medium heat for about 10 minutes, until the apples have broken down. Leave to cool, then stir in the calvados, if using.

Preheat your oven to 190°C/170°C fan/375°F/Gas 5.

Flatten the bread slices with a rolling pin until about 2mm/¹∕₁₆in thick. Cut one slice into a circle the same size as the base of the pudding bowl. Dip the circle of bread into the melted butter and place it at the bottom of the bowl.

Put one of the remaining slices of bread to one side and slice the rest in half lengthways. Dip each strip into the melted butter and use the strips to line the inside of the bowl, making sure the next strip overlaps the previous until you have completely covered the inside. Leave a small overhang at the lip, if possible.

Spoon the apple filling into the pudding bowl so that it comes right to the top. Press it down to ensure there are no gaps.

Dip the reserved slice of bread into the melted butter and use this slice to cover the apple filling, pinching the bread around the rim of the bowl to seal. Place the bowl in a baking tin and into the oven. Bake the pudding for about 40 minutes, until golden and crisp on top, then leave it to cool for 10 minutes.

Meanwhile, make the sweet cream. Whip the cream with the icing sugar and vanilla in a bowl to soft peaks. Set aside.

Place a serving plate on top of the pudding bowl and invert the pudding out on to the plate. Remove the bowl to reveal the pudding. Serve with spoonfuls of the sweet cream alongside.

# SLOE GIN JELLIES WITH BLACKBERRIES & CREAM

60g/2¼oz/scant ⅓ cup caster
    (superfine) sugar
finely grated zest and juice
    of 1 orange
6 gelatine leaves
200ml/7fl oz/generous ¾ cup
    sloe gin
400ml/14fl oz/1¾ cups prosecco
    or any sparkling white wine
300g/10½oz/2¼ cups blackberries
150ml/5fl oz/⅔ cup whipping cream

You will need 4 wine glasses
or individual serving bowls.

SERVES | TOTAL TIME TO MAKE
4 | 02 HOURS | 20 MINS

Having begun life as a poor relation to the far more sophisticated port, by the turn of the 20th century, sloe gin was distilled in its own right and its reputation began to take an upturn. By the 1920s, at society events such as Derby Day, sloe gin fizz would have been the cocktail of choice. Here, that cocktail comes as a jelly for a fitting lunchtime dessert at the races.

Pour 150ml/5fl oz/⅔ cup of water into a medium saucepan. Add 50g/1¾oz/¼ cup of the sugar and all the orange juice and warm the mixture through over a medium heat until the sugar has dissolved. Remove from the heat and set aside.

Soften the gelatine leaves in cold water for 5 minutes. Remove the leaves and squeeze out the excess water. Stir the gelatine into the orange syrup in the pan. Pour the syrup into a jug and add 175ml/5¾fl oz/¾ cup of the sloe gin. Leave to go cold, then stir in the prosecco or sparkling wine and mix well. Leave the jelly to settle so that there are no air bubbles.

Pour the jelly into 4 glasses or individual serving bowls and transfer them to the fridge. Refrigerate for about 2 hours, until each jelly has a perfect, wobbly set.

When you're ready to serve, place the blackberries (halve them if they are large) into a bowl, sprinkle over the remaining caster sugar and sloe gin and toss to coat. Whip the cream in a bowl to soft peaks. Top each jelly with equal amounts of the flavoured blackberries and serve each with a dollop of whipped cream.

# DINNER AT THE EDEN CLUB

# LUXURY CHEESE & ONION STRAWS

225g/8oz/1¾ cups plain
   (all-purpose) flour
100g/3½oz/½ cup minus
   1 tablespoon butter,
   cubed and chilled
3 thyme sprigs, leaves picked
   and chopped
2 teaspoons wholegrain mustard
¼ teaspoon smoked paprika
150g/5½oz extra-mature
   Cheddar, grated
2 spring onions (scallions),
   finely chopped
1 egg yolk
1 egg, beaten
2 teaspoons poppy seeds
2 teaspoons sesame seeds
salt and ground black pepper

**We've made these cheese straws using Cheddar, but you could substitute any cheese you prefer – Parmesan would work a treat and Darby Sabini would definitely approve! Serve them up with something fizzy as a pre-dinner nibble.**

Preheat your oven to 200°C/180°C fan/400°F/Gas 6 and line two baking trays with baking paper.

Tip the flour into a mixing bowl and add the butter, rubbing it in with your fingertips until the mixture resembles breadcrumbs. Add the thyme, mustard, smoked paprika, Cheddar and spring onions, season well with salt and pepper and mix to combine.

Add the egg yolk and, using a round-bladed knife, bring the mixture together to form a dough. If it feels too dry, add 1 tablespoon of cold water. Roll out the dough on a lightly floured surface to a 20cm/8in square, about 1cm/½in thick.

Cut the dough lengthways into 20 strips, each about 1cm/½in wide. Brush the strips with the beaten egg and sprinkle them with the poppy and sesame seeds. Place the strips on to the lined baking trays, leaving a little room between each.

Bake for 12–15 minutes, until golden brown, then remove the straws from the oven and leave them to cool slightly on the baking trays, then transfer to a wire rack to cool completely.

MAKES | TOTAL TIME TO MAKE
20 | 00 HOURS | 35 MINS

# BLUE CHEESE FILO TARTLETS

4 sheets of filo pastry (each about
    48 x 25cm/19 x 10in)
a knob of butter, melted
12 teaspoons fig chutney
150g/5½oz blue cheese
    (Stilton, Roquefort or
    Gorgonzola work beautifully)
200ml/7fl oz/generous ¾ cup
    double (heavy) cream
2 eggs
¼ bunch of chives, finely chopped
1 ripe conference pear
a squeeze of lemon juice
5 walnut halves, finely chopped
salt and ground black pepper
a handful of watercress, to serve

You will need a 12-cup non-stick
or lightly oiled muffin tin.

MAKES · TOTAL TIME TO MAKE
12 · 00 HOURS · 45 MINS

These wonderful little tarts, baked in a muffin tin, make an ideal appetizer, or a light starter served with watercress salad on the side. Use vegetarian blue cheese if you're looking for a meat-free option.

Preheat your oven to 180°C/160°C fan/350°F/Gas 4.

Brush 1 sheet of filo pastry all over with melted butter. Lay a second sheet on top and brush that with butter, too. Turn the stacked sheets so that a short end is closest to you and slice down the middle, top to bottom to give two long halves. Cut across the narrow width at one third and two thirds of the way down to give 6 equal portions of double-layer filo. Place 1 portion into each of 6 hollows in the muffin tin, leaving a small overhang. Repeat with the remaining 2 sheets of filo, so that all 12 cups are lined with pastry.

Spoon 1 teaspoon of chutney into each filo case, then crumble in equal amounts of the blue cheese. Set aside.

In a bowl, beat together the cream and eggs, seasoning with a little salt and black pepper, then stir in half the chives.

Divide the cream mixture between each pastry case and bake the tartlets for about 20 minutes, until the pastry is golden and crunchy and the filling is cooked through.

While the tartlets are baking, peel, core and chop the pear into small pieces. Pop the pieces into a bowl and stir through the squeeze of lemon juice. Add the walnuts and combine.

Once the tartlets are ready, remove them from the muffin tin and transfer them to a serving plate (you may need to leave them to cool a little first). Top each with the pear and walnut mixture, then sprinkle with the remaining chives. Serve warm or cold with a few watercress leaves.

# LOBSTER CROQUETTES

MAKES **12**
TOTAL TIME TO MAKE **01** HOURS **30** MINS

a knob of butter
3 tablespoons plain (all-purpose) flour
150ml/5fl oz/²⁄₃ cup full-fat milk
generous 1 tablespoon double (heavy) cream
1 teaspoon English mustard
100g/3½oz cooked mashed potato
a handful of flat-leaf parsley, leaves picked and chopped, plus optional extra to serve
250g/9oz cooked lobster meat, roughly chopped
vegetable oil, for deep-frying
salt and ground black pepper

### FOR THE COATING

50–70g/1¾–2½oz/generous ⅓–generous ½ cup plain (all-purpose) flour
1 egg, beaten with 100ml/3½fl oz/ generous ⅓ cup full-fat milk
100g/3½oz/2 cups panko breadcrumbs

### FOR THE DIP

3 tablespoons mayonnaise
1 tablespoon tomato ketchup
finely grated zest of 1 lemon
1 tablespoon capers, chopped
4–5 dill fronds, leaves picked and chopped

If you don't fancy lobster, you can use chopped, cooked prawns for the croquette filling instead.

**The sweetness of British lobster lends itself particularly well to these delicious croquettes, which make a decadent appetizer with a pre-dinner cocktail or glass of Champagne.**

Melt the butter in a small saucepan over a medium heat. Add the flour and cook, stirring, for 1 minute. A little at a time, add the milk, stirring continuously as you do so. Once you have added all the milk, add the cream, mustard, mashed potato and parsley, and give it all a good stir. Season with salt and pepper, remove from the heat and pour the mixture into a bowl to cool completely.

Fold the lobster into the cooled mixture, then cover the bowl and leave the mixture in the fridge for about 1 hour, to firm up.

With damp hands, take about 2 tablespoons of the mixture and form it into a cylinder. Place the formed croquette filling on to a tray and repeat until you have used up all the mixture. You should have enough mixture to make 12 croquettes altogether.

To coat, tip the flour into a wide, shallow bowl, then add the egg mixture to another and the breadcrumbs to a third.

One by one, gently dip the cylinders into the flour, turning them to coat, then into the egg and then into the breadcrumbs. Place the croquettes back on to the tray as you go. (At this stage, you can refrigerate the croquettes for frying later, if you like.)

If you have a deep-fat fryer, heat the oil to 180°C/350°F. If not, one third fill a medium saucepan with vegetable oil and place it over a medium heat. The oil is ready when the temperature reaches 180°C/350°F on a digital cooking thermometer, or when a cube of bread floats and browns within 30 seconds.

Deep-fry the croquettes, in batches of about 6 at a time, for about 2 minutes, moving them around, until golden and crisp. Remove each batch with a slotted spoon and set the croquettes aside to drain on kitchen paper while you deep-fry the remainder.

Make the dip by simply mixing the ingredients together and popping it into a serving dish. Arrange the croquettes on a serving platter with the dip and serve sprinkled with a little extra chopped parsley, if you like.

# PAN-FRIED SIRLOIN STEAKS WITH GAME CHIPS & CHEESY PORTOBELLO MUSHROOMS

2 portobello mushrooms
large knob of butter,
    at room temperature
2 garlic cloves, thinly sliced
1 thyme sprig, leaves picked
100g/3½oz baby spinach
50g/1¾oz blue stilton, crumbled
2 tablespoons double (heavy) cream
2 tablespoons panko breadcrumbs
2 sirloin steaks (about 225g/8oz each)
1 tablespoon olive oil
salt and ground black pepper
English mustard, to serve (optional)

## FOR THE GAME CHIPS

200g/7oz potatoes
    (such as maris piper)
1 parsnip
vegetable oil, for deep-frying
3 rosemary sprigs, leaves picked
    and roughly chopped
1 teaspoon sweet paprika
½ teaspoon sea salt

SERVES **2** | TOTAL TIME TO MAKE **00** HOURS **50** MINS

**Steak, mushroom and chips, Eden Club-style. This far more sophisticated take on the classic includes game chips — so-called because they used to be served alongside rich-tasting game meats.**

Preheat your oven to 190°C/170°C fan/375°F/Gas 5.

Place the mushrooms into a small baking dish. Using one third of the butter, spread a little butter over each mushroom. Top with the sliced garlic and the thyme leaves and bake for 5 minutes, until the garlic has softened. Remove from the oven and set aside.

Meanwhile, in a small saucepan, cook the spinach in the remaining butter over a medium heat for 1 minute, until wilted. Press out any excess water, then divide the spinach between the 2 mushrooms. Scatter over the stilton, add a tablespoon of cream to each and sprinkle over the breadcrumbs. Return the mushrooms to the oven and bake for 5 minutes, until the cheese has melted and the breadcrumbs are golden. Turn the oven off, but leave the mushrooms inside to stay warm.

Make the game chips. Peel the potatoes and parsnip or keep the skins on, as you prefer. Slice the potatoes thinly using a mandolin or very sharp knife and place them into a bowl of cold water for 10 minutes. Drain well on kitchen paper. Thinly slice the parsnips and set those aside on kitchen paper, too.

If you have a deep-fat fryer, heat the oil to 190°C/375°F. If not, one third fill a medium saucepan with vegetable oil and place it over a medium heat. The oil is ready when the temperature reaches 190°C/375°F on a digital cooking thermometer, or when a cube of bread floats and browns within 25–30 seconds. Deep-fry the potatoes and parsnips in 3 or 4 batches for about 5 minutes per batch, turning occasionally, until crisp. Drain on kitchen paper, then toss the chips in a baking tray with the rosemary, paprika and salt and pop them in the residual heat of the oven to keep warm.

Season the steaks with salt and pepper and brush them with the olive oil. Heat a frying pan or griddle over a medium–high heat until hot. Add the steaks and cook for 2½ minutes on each side for medium–rare, 3½ minutes for medium and 5 minutes for well done. Remove from the heat and leave the steaks to rest in the pan for a few minutes before serving with the game chips and mushrooms, and some English mustard, if you wish.

# STEAMED SOLE FILLETS WITH BROWN SHRIMPS & SAMPHIRE IN A PARCEL

1 courgette (zucchini), sliced
200g/7oz new potatoes,
    boiled, cooled and sliced
½ lemon, sliced
10 cherry tomatoes
4 skinless, boneless lemon
    or dover sole fillets
    (about 75g/2½oz each)
25g/1oz samphire
50g/1¾oz brown shrimps
2 teaspoons capers
4 dill fronds
2 tarragon sprigs
a knob of butter
100ml/3½fl oz/generous ⅓ cup
    dry white wine
salt and ground black pepper

**The 'en papillotte' (in paper) cooking technique in this recipe locks flavour inside the parcel, producing a complete meal of tender vegetables topped with lovely, moist fish.**

Preheat your oven to 200°C/180°C fan/400°F/Gas 6 and cut two pieces of baking paper each to a 30cm/12in square.

Place equal amounts of the courgette, potatoes and lemon slightly to one side of each square of baking paper. Top with the cherry tomatoes. Place the fish fillets on top of the tomatoes, then scatter over the samphire, brown shrimps and capers and then the dill and tarragon. Season with salt and pepper and top with the butter. Scrunch the sides of the paper so that each parcel will hold a little liquid and pour equal amounts of the wine into each parcel.

Take one edge of the paper and fold it over the contents of the parcel to meet the other edge. Fold and pleat or scrunch the edges together, much as if you were making a Cornish pasty, to seal in all the ingredients and ensure that no steam can escape. Place the parcels on a baking tray and bake the fish for 10–12 minutes, until the parcels puff up and start to brown a little. Serve straight away (parcels and all), for a gift of a meal, unwrapped at the table.

SERVES | TOTAL TIME TO MAKE
2 | 00 HOURS | 25 MINS

# LAMB CUTLETS IN ROSEMARY, ANCHOVY & CAPER BUTTER WITH SLOW-BRAISED LEEKS

75g/2½oz/⅓ cup butter,
    at room temperature
5 salted anchovy fillets,
    very finely chopped
1 tablespoon capers,
    very finely chopped
a handful of flat-leaf parsley,
    leaves picked and very
    finely chopped
50g/1¾oz/⅓ cup toasted
    hazelnuts, finely chopped
4 rosemary sprigs, leaves picked
    and very finely chopped, plus
    optional extra sprigs to garnish
8 lamb cutlets (or chops, if you prefer)
2 tablespoons olive oil
salt and ground black pepper
buttery mashed potato, to serve

## FOR THE LEEKS

a knob of butter
3 leeks, white parts cut into
    6cm/2½in lengths, green
    tops finely chopped
2 garlic cloves, thinly sliced
100ml/3½fl oz/generous ⅓ cup
    dry white wine
200ml/7fl oz/generous ¾ cup
    vegetable stock
5 thyme sprigs, leaves picked
    and chopped
200g/7oz/generous 1½ cups
    frozen peas
a small handful of mint,
    leaves picked and chopped
100ml/3½fl oz/generous ⅓ cup
    double (heavy) cream

**Sophisticated crusted cutlets with rich and creamy braised leeks – this is late-night jazz club food to eat with a glass of full-bodied red wine and the soft, deep, reassuring drum of the music.**

Put the butter into a bowl. Add the anchovies, capers, parsley, hazelnuts and half the rosemary and mix well. Lay a large piece of baking paper on your work surface. Place the flavoured butter in the middle, roll it into a sausage shape about 10–12cm/4–4½in long (use the baking paper to help you), wrap it, and place it in the fridge to firm up until needed.

Next, make the leeks. Melt the butter in a large frying pan with a lid, over a medium heat. Add the pieces of white leek and fry for about 8–10 minutes, keeping the leeks moving in the pan so that they don't catch, until they start to soften and brown a little. Add the garlic and green parts of the leeks and cook for 3–4 minutes. Pour in the white wine and leave it to bubble for 3 minutes, then add the vegetable stock and thyme leaves. Pop on the lid, reduce the heat to a simmer and cook for 25 minutes, then add the peas. Cook for 5 minutes more to heat them through, then stir through the mint and cream.

While the leeks are braising, cook the lamb. Place the lamb cutlets on to a large grill pan, season them with salt and pepper, drizzle over the olive oil and scatter over the remaining rosemary. Leave for 15 minutes at room temperature. Meanwhile, preheat your grill to medium–high.

Remove the butter from the fridge and slice it into eight 1cm/½in disks (if you have extra, you can freeze it to use another day).

Place the lamb cutlets under the hot grill and grill them for 2–3 minutes on the first side, then turn them over and grill them for another 2–3 minutes on the other side. Remove the cutlets from the grill and top each with a disk of butter, leaving the butter to melt a little. Serve the lamb cutlets, garnished with a few extra rosemary sprigs if you wish, with the braised leeks and a big bowl of buttery mash.

SERVES **4** | TOTAL TIME TO MAKE **01** HOUR **10** MINS

# OLD ENGLISH FISH PIE

50g/1¾oz/3½ tablespoons butter
1 large leek, roughly chopped
50g/1¾oz/generous ⅓ cup plain
    (all-purpose) flour
600ml/21fl oz/2½ cups full-fat milk
4 blocks of frozen spinach
½ teaspoon English mustard
a handful of flat-leaf parsley,
    leaves picked and chopped
4 tarragon sprigs, leaves picked
    and roughly chopped
300g/10½oz skinless,
    boneless salmon fillet, cut
    into 3–4cm/1¼–1½in dice
1 large skinless, boneless smoked
    haddock fillet (about 250g/9oz),
    cut into 3–4cm/1¼–1½in dice
200g/7oz skinless, boneless whiting,
    cod or any other white fish fillet,
    cut into 3–4cm/1¼–1½in dice
200g/7oz cooked, peeled baby prawns
4 hard-boiled eggs, peeled and
    roughly chopped
steamed seasonal green
    vegetables, to serve

### FOR THE TOPPING

1kg/2lb 4oz potatoes (such as maris
    piper), peeled and chopped into
    5cm/2in chunks
75g/2½oz/⅓ cup butter
3 spring onions (scallions), chopped
150ml/5fl oz/⅔ cup full-fat milk
100g/3½oz/2 cups panko breadcrumbs
50g/1¾oz mature Cheddar, grated
salt and ground black pepper

You will need a 25 x 30cm/10 x 12in
oven dish.

**Under new management, we think the Eden Club might serve up something particularly British and hearty – like this fish pie. Although, not for long, of course, before the Italians take over again.**

First, start the topping. Boil the potatoes in a large pan of salted water for 20–25 minutes, until tender. Drain them in a colander and leave them to steam dry. Meanwhile, melt the butter in the same pan over a medium heat. Add the spring onions and milk and bring the milk to a simmer. Remove from the heat and tip in the potatoes. Season with salt and pepper and mash until smooth. Set aside.

For the filling, melt the butter in a medium saucepan over a medium heat. Add the leek and fry for 5–7 minutes, until soft. Stir in the flour and, once it's incorporated, add the milk, a little at a time, beating continuously with a wooden spoon. Make sure the mixture is smooth between each addition. When you have added all the milk and have a silky-smooth sauce, stir in the frozen spinach, and the mustard, parsley and tarragon. Leave to one side.

Preheat your oven to 190°C/170°C fan/375°F/Gas 5.

Place the diced salmon, smoked haddock and white fish into the base of your oven dish. Sprinkle over the prawns and eggs. Pour over the sauce making sure the fish is completely covered. Spoon the mash over the top and smooth out the surface into an even layer, then run a fork through it to create some lumps and bumps. Sprinkle over the breadcrumbs and the grated cheese to finish the topping.

Bake the fish pie for about 40 minutes, until the fish is cooked through, the sauce is bubbling and the top is golden and crisp. Serve with steamed seasonal green vegetables.

SERVES | TOTAL TIME TO MAKE
6 | 01 HOUR | 25 MINS

# GAMEKEEPER'S PIE

2 tablespoons plain (all-purpose) flour
250g/9oz venison haunch, diced
3 tablespoons vegetable oil
400g/14oz diced mixed game
     (such as pheasant, partridge,
     pigeon, rabbit)
100g/3½oz smoked bacon lardons
100g/3½oz shallots, halved
150g/5½oz chestnut
     mushrooms, halved
250ml/9fl oz/generous 1 cup red wine
300ml/10½fl oz/1¼ cups chicken stock
3 tablespoons Worcestershire sauce
5 fresh or vacuum-packed
     chestnuts, chopped
2 rosemary sprigs, plus a few picked
     and chopped leaves for sprinkling
2 thyme sprigs, plus a few picked
     leaves for sprinkling
2 bay leaves
1 tablespoon redcurrant jelly
100ml/3½fl oz/generous ⅓ cup
     double (heavy) cream
200g/7oz potatoes (such as maris
     piper), peeled and cut into
     3mm/⅛in slices
1 small celeriac (celery root), peeled
     and cut into 3mm/⅛in slices
2 large beetroots (beets), peeled
     and cut into 3mm/⅛in slices
1 small swede, peeled and cut
     into 3mm/⅛in slices
a knob of butter
salt and ground black pepper
pickled red cabbage, to serve

**Hunting for game was an activity that transcended the social classes. As well as the venison, you can use whichever small game your butcher has available for this indulgent, warming game pie. We've topped it with sliced potatoes, but mash or pastry would work well, instead, if you prefer.**

Preheat your oven to 150°C/130°C fan/300°F/Gas 2.

Tip the flour into a mixing bowl and season it generously with salt and pepper. Toss the venison in the seasoned flour.

Heat 1 tablespoon of the vegetable oil in a large casserole pan over a high heat and add the venison, shaking off any excess flour (reserve the flour). Fry for 5–7 minutes, stirring occasionally, until browned all over. Remove from the pan with a slotted spoon and set aside. Add another tablespoon of the oil to the pan and while it heats up, toss the game mixture in the seasoned flour. Transfer this to the pan and fry for 5–7 minutes, turning, until browned. Remove from the pan and set aside with the venison. Add the remaining oil to the pan, then add the bacon and shallots. Fry for 7–8 minutes, stirring, until the shallots are browned and the bacon crisps.

Return the venison and game to the pan and add the mushrooms. Cook for 2–3 minutes, then pour in the red wine, chicken stock and Worcestershire sauce and bring it to a simmer. Add the chestnuts, rosemary and thyme sprigs and bay leaves, pop the lid on the pan and place the stew into the oven for 1 hour, then remove it from the oven and increase the oven temperature to 180°C/160°C fan/350°F/Gas 4.

Stir the redcurrant jelly and cream into the stew, then cover the surface with the slices of potato, celeriac, beetroot and swede. Dot with the butter, season the topping with salt and pepper and sprinkle with the extra herbs. Place the pie back in the oven (without the lid) for 35 minutes, until the vegetables are tender and the topping is starting to crisp. Serve with pickled red cabbage.

SERVES | TOTAL TIME TO MAKE
6 | 02 HOURS | 15 MINS

# GENTLEMAN'S PUDDING WITH RASPBERRY SAUCE & CUSTARD

150g/5½oz/⅔ cup butter,
    at room temperature
6 tablespoons caster
    (superfine) sugar
3 eggs
150g/5½oz/generous 1 cup
    self-raising flour, sifted
finely grated zest of 1 lemon
3 tablespoons raspberry jam (jelly)
a couple of handfuls of fresh
    raspberries or a few spoonfuls
    of jam (jelly), to serve (optional)

## FOR THE CUSTARD

4 egg yolks
2 tablespoons caster
    (superfine) sugar
1 teaspoon vanilla extract
3½ tablespoons full-fat milk
3–4 tablespoons brandy

You will need a 1 litre/35fl oz
pudding bowl, greased with
butter, and a ramekin.

| SERVES | TOTAL TIME TO MAKE | |
| --- | --- | --- |
| 6 | 01 HOUR | 20 MINS |

**There's nothing very gentlemanly about the way the Peaky Blinders take control of the Eden Club. If you don't fancy brandy in your custard, whiskey or spiced rum would work just as well.**

Upturn a ramekin and place it in the bottom of a large saucepan with a lid. This is going to be your steamer.

Using an electric hand whisk, beat the butter and sugar together until very light and pale – almost mousse-like. Add 1 egg and 1 tablespoon of the flour and whisk again. Add a second egg and another tablespoon of flour, whisk, then add the last egg and another tablespoon of the flour and whisk again. Fold in the last of the flour and add the lemon zest. Now stir in the jam, but not to combine – just so you have a ripple effect.

Pour the batter into the prepared pudding bowl. Cover the top with a disk of baking paper to that the paper overhangs the sides of the bowl and secure it round the rim with string. Place the pudding into the pan, on top of the ramekin. Pour in cold water so that it comes almost to the base of the pudding bowl and place the pan over a low heat with the lid on. Steam the pudding for about 1 hour, until cooked through (check the water level from time to time and top up with boiling water if the pan looks a bit dry).

Once the pudding has been steaming for about 50 minutes, start the custard. Place the egg yolks, sugar and vanilla into a heat-resistant bowl set over a small pan of simmering water. Make sure the water does not come into contact with the base of the bowl. Whisk the egg mixture over the water until it's light, fluffy and thickened (about 5 minutes). Whisk in the milk and then the brandy until combined. Remove the bowl from the heat and pour the custard into a jug.

Remove the pudding bowl from the pan, untie the string and remove the baking paper. Place a serving plate on top of the bowl, and, protecting your hands with a towel, invert the pudding on to the plate. Serve with the custard and a few fresh raspberries or spoonfuls of jam, too, if you like.

# THE FEAST AT ARROW HOUSE

# MENU

SERVES 6

**A Selection of Arrow House Canapés**

..........................

ENTRÉE
**Pea & Lettuce Soup with Feta**
OR
**Chicken & Pork Terrine with Brandy & Apricots**

..........................

MAIN COURSE
**Wild Mushroom, Chard & Beetroot Tart**
OR
**Rack of Lamb with a Mustard & Whiskey Glaze & Caper Sauce**
OR
**Butter & Sage Roast Chicken with Mushrooms & Tarragon Cream Sauce**

..........................

DESSERT
**Vanilla Custard Tart with Roasted Gooseberries**
OR
**Summer Pudding with Gin-infused Berries**

..........................

**Digestifs**

..........................

CARRIAGES AT MIDNIGHT

# CANAPÉS

Welcome to dinner. Try these as you sip your apéritifs — a fine selection of Arrow House 'savouries', highly seasoned canapés that offer just two or three delicate mouthfuls to whet your appetite before you sit down for the main event.

1 part-baked baguette,
    cut into 1cm/½in slices
2 tablespoons olive oil
300g/10½oz piece of beef fillet
2 cooked pickled beetroot (beets),
    finely chopped
3 gherkins, finely chopped
a small handful of watercress,
    half roughly chopped
200ml/7fl oz/generous ¾ cup
    double (heavy) cream
1 teaspoon wholegrain mustard
¼ bunch of chives, chopped
salt and ground black pepper

MAKES **18** | TOTAL TIME TO MAKE **00** HOURS **20** MINS

## RARE BEEF FILLET CROSTINI WITH MUSTARD & WATERCRESS

Preheat your oven to 190°C/170°C fan/375°F/Gas 5. Place the baguette slices on a baking sheet. Brush each slice with some of the olive oil and season with a little salt and pepper. Bake for 5 minutes, until golden, then leave to cool.

Place the beef between two pieces of baking paper and flatten it to about 3–4cm/1¼–1½in thick. Season with salt and pepper and drizzle over the remaining oil. Heat a frying pan over a medium–high heat and cook the beef for 2 minutes each side. Leave to rest.

Combine the beetroot and gherkins in a bowl. Place the chopped watercress into a separate bowl with the cream and mustard, season with salt and pepper and whisk until thickened.

Spread a little of the mustard cream on to each mini toast and add a little of the remaining watercress. Thinly slice the beef and divide it between the toasts. Top with the beetroot mixture and finish with a sprinkling of chopped chives.

75g/2½oz/⅓ full-fat cream cheese
150g/5½oz hot smoked salmon
50g/1¾oz cold smoked salmon,
    chopped into small pieces
3½ tablespoons double (heavy) cream
juice of ½ lemon
1 teaspoon horseradish sauce
1–2 dill sprigs, fronds picked and finely
    chopped, plus extra to garnish
½ cucumber, very thinly sliced
1 tablespoon white wine vinegar
½ tablespoon caster (superfine) sugar
3 slices of rye bread, lightly toasted
salt and ground black pepper

MAKES **12** | TOTAL TIME TO MAKE **00** HOURS **15** MINS

## SMOKED SALMON MOUSSE TOASTS WITH PICKLED CUCUMBER

Place the cream cheese in bowl. Flake over the hot smoked salmon and, using a fork, mix until well combined. Add the cold smoked salmon, cream, lemon juice, horseradish sauce and dill and season with salt and pepper. Mix to combine, then cover and refrigerate until needed.

Put the cucumber slices in a bowl and sprinkle over a little salt. Leave for 5 minutes, then squeeze out any excess water and pop the slices in a bowl with the vinegar and sugar. Toss together, leave for another 5 minutes, then drain.

Cut the crusts off the toasted rye bread and cut the slices into smallish squares, to give 12 pieces altogether (or stamp out small circles, if you have a suitably sized cutter).

Either spoon the mousse into a piping bag fitted with a large open star nozzle and pipe the salmon mousse on top of each slice of toast, or use two spoons to do the job. Add some pickled cucumber to each slice, then finish with a little chopped dill.

1 x 500g/1lb 2oz block of puff pastry
plain (all-purpose) flour, for dusting
1 egg, beaten

### FOR THE CURRIED CHICKEN FILLING

2 tablespoons mayonnaise
1 teaspoon mild curry powder
¼ teaspoon chilli powder (optional)
2 teaspoons mango chutney
1 celery stalk, finely chopped
20g/¾oz sultanas (golden raisins)
a small handful of flat-leaf parsley,
    leaves picked and chopped
150g/5½oz cooked chicken meat,
    finely chopped
25g/1oz/⅓ cup flaked (slivered)
    almonds, lightly toasted

### FOR THE PICKLED WALNUT
### & BLUE CHEESE FILLING

100g/3½oz favourite blue cheese
    (stilton, castello blue, roquefort
    or saint agur are good)
100ml/3½fl oz/generous ⅓ cup
    double (heavy) cream
2 teaspoons cranberry sauce
2 pickled walnuts, finely chopped
3 sprigs of flat-leaf parsley,
    leaves picked and chopped
salt and ground black pepper

### FOR THE PRAWNS WITH
### SPICY MAYO FILLING

2 tablespoons mayonnaise
1 teaspoon tomato ketchup
¼ teaspoon cayenne pepper
2 dashes of Worcestershire sauce
a squeeze of lemon juice
200g/7oz cooked, peeled baby
    prawns (shrimp)
sweet paprika, for sprinkling
a small handful of flat-leaf parsley,
    leaves picked and chopped

You will need 6–7cm/2½–2¾in
and 4cm/1½in fluted pastry cutters.

# VOL AU VENTS THREE WAYS

Line a baking sheet with baking paper.

Roll out the pastry on a lightly floured surface to a rectangle about 35 x 25cm/14 x 10in and about 5mm/¼in thick. Using the larger pastry cutter, stamp out 24 disks, re-rolling the trimmings as necessary. Place half the disks on the lined baking sheet and prick them all over with a fork. Brush with beaten egg.

Using a 4cm/1½in cutter, stamp out the middle from the remaining disks. Discard the pastry from the middles, bring the trimmings together and freeze the pastry for another day.

Place the pastry rings on top of the glazed pastry disks, gently pressing them together. Brush the tops with beaten egg, then chill the unbaked cases for 20 minutes to firm up. Meanwhile, preheat your oven to 200°C/180°C fan/400°F/Gas 6.

Bake the chilled cases for 15–20 minutes, until puffed up and golden. Leave to cool completely before filling.

While the cases are chilling, make the fillings. Start with the curried chicken – simply mix everything together except the flaked almonds and set aside.

For the pickled walnut and blue cheese filling, crumble the cheese into a bowl. Add the cream and season with a little salt and pepper. Beat the mixture together with a wooden spoon until smooth. Set aside.

To make the prawns with spicy mayo filling, combine the mayonnaise, tomato ketchup, cayenne pepper, Worcestershire sauce and lemon juice in a bowl. Season with salt and pepper, then fold in the prawns.

When the pastry cases have cooled, spoon the curried chicken into 4 of the cases and top them equally with the toasted flaked almonds. To finish the pickled walnut and blue cheese vol au vents, add ½ teaspoon of cranberry sauce to 4 of the vol au vent cases, then spoon or pipe in the blue cheese mixture. Combine the walnuts and parsley in a small bowl and spoon this on top of the filling. Finally, spoon the prawn mixture into the remaining 4 cases. Sprinkle a little paprika and parsley over the top of these to finish.

MAKES | TOTAL TIME TO MAKE
12 | 00 HOURS | 40 MINS

# PEA & LETTUCE SOUP WITH FETA

a knob of butter
1 leek, chopped
1 celery stalk, chopped
2 garlic cloves, chopped
1 litre/35fl oz/generous
    4 cups vegetable stock
2 all-rounder potatoes,
    peeled and chopped
1 baby gem lettuce,
    roughly chopped
250g/9oz/2 cups frozen peas
a small handful of mint,
    leaves picked and chopped
60g/2¼oz feta, crumbled
¼ bunch of chives or 5–6 dill
    fronds, finely chopped
3½ tablespoons single (light) cream
extra-virgin olive oil, for drizzling
salt and ground black pepper
crusty bread, to serve

**The feta cheese sprinkled over this soup gives a salty, tangy edge to the creamy, mellow pea. For supper at Arrow House, the Shelbys are serving this hot, but you could just as well chill it and serve it as a gazpacho.**

Melt the butter in a saucepan over a medium–low heat. Add the leek, celery and garlic and fry for 10 minutes, until softened.

Pour in the vegetable stock, add the potatoes and bring the liquid to a simmer. Simmer, uncovered, for 10 minutes, then add the lettuce, peas and mint. Continue cooking for a further 5 minutes, then blend until smooth. Taste and season the soup with salt and pepper.

Divide the soup equally between the serving bowls. Sprinkle a little feta into each bowl and sprinkle the chopped herbs on top. Finish with a drizzle of cream and extra-virgin olive oil. Serve with crusty bread.

SERVES | TOTAL TIME TO MAKE
6 | 00 HOURS | 40 MINS

# CHICKEN & PORK TERRINE WITH BRANDY & APRICOTS

12 rashers of unsmoked streaky bacon
50g/1¾oz/3½ tablespoons butter
1 large onion, finely chopped
5 garlic cloves, crushed
400g/14oz chicken livers
1 egg, beaten
50g/1¾oz/1 cup fresh breadcrumbs
2 tablespoons brandy
8 thyme sprigs, leaves picked
2 skinless, boneless chicken breasts,
    cut into 2–3cm/¾–1¼in cubes
400g/14oz pork belly, skin removed,
    flesh diced
10 dried pitted apricots, chopped
a handful of flat-leaf parsley, leaves
    picked and chopped
5 sage leaves, chopped
boiling water from a kettle
salt and ground black pepper

## TO SERVE

your favourite chutney
18 cornichons
3 handfuls of watercress
6 slices of wholegrain bread,
    toasted and buttered

You will need a 900g/2lb loaf tin,
lined with a double layer of cling
film with plenty of overhang,
and another loaf tin to weigh
down the terrine.

SERVES | TOTAL TIME TO MAKE
10 | 02 HOURS | 10 MINS

**Wrapped in bacon and with distinct layers, this terrine looks far harder to achieve than it is. Definitely one to impress the guests.**

Using the back of a knife, stretch out the bacon rashers to make them as long as possible. Use the lengthened rashers to line the loaf tin across its narrow width, slightly overlapping the rashers and making sure you leave an overhang.

Melt the butter in a medium saucepan over a low heat. Add the onion and fry for 5–7 minutes, until translucent but not coloured. Add the garlic and cook for 1 minute to soften. Cool completely.

Tip the cooled onion and garlic mixture into a food processor with 300g/10½oz of the chicken livers and blend until smooth. Roughly chop the remaining chicken livers.

Tip the blitzed mixture into a mixing bowl. Stir in the chopped livers, along with the egg, breadcrumbs, brandy and thyme leaves and season generously with salt and pepper. Set aside.

Put the chicken, pork and apricots in a separate bowl and add the parsley and sage. Season with salt and pepper and combine.

Preheat your oven to 160°C/140°C fan/320°F/Gas 2½.

Spread one third of the chicken liver mixture over the base of the lined tin, smoothing it out in an even layer. Top with half the chicken and pork mixture, again creating an even layer. Add another third of the chicken liver mixture, then the remaining diced chicken and pork. Finish with a smooth, even layer of the remaining liver.

Fold the overhanging strips of bacon over to encase the filling. Fold over the cling film and wrap the whole tin in a double layer of foil, sealing the edges tightly. Place the terrine into a deep-sided roasting tin, pour boiling water into the tray until it comes half way up the sides of the terrine, and place the whole thing into the oven. Bake for 1½ hours, until the layers are completely cooked through.

Remove the terrine from the water bath. Place another loaf tin on top of it and weigh it down with a couple of cans of beans or another heavy weight. When the tin is cold, transfer it to the fridge (with the weights) to chill overnight.

To serve, unwrap the terrine and invert it out on to a serving plate. Cut it into slices and serve it with a favourite chutney, a few cornichons, a little watercress, and buttered toast on the side. Any leftover terrine will keep, covered, in the fridge for 5 days.

# MUSHROOM, CHARD & BEETROOT TART

1 x 500g/1lb 2oz block of
    shortcrust pastry
plain (all-purpose) flour, for dusting
10 thyme sprigs, leaves picked
50g/1¾oz/3½ tablespoons butter
200g/7oz rainbow chard, leaves
    chopped into 2–3cm/¾–1¼in
    pieces, stalks reserved
    and chopped
3 cooked, peeled beetroots
    (beets; not pickled), chopped
3 eggs
200ml/7fl oz/generous ¾ cup
    double (heavy) cream
100ml/3½fl oz/generous ⅓ cup
    full-fat milk
50g/1¾oz Parmesan, grated
250g/9oz mixed mushrooms,
    roughly chopped into
    bitesize pieces
3 garlic cloves, sliced
10 walnut halves, chopped
a handful of watercress,
    roughly chopped, plus
    extra leaves to serve
salt and ground black pepper

You will need a 23cm/9in
loose-bottomed tart tin,
greased and floured.

| SERVES | TOTAL TIME TO MAKE | |
| --- | --- | --- |
| 6 | 01 HOUR | 40 MINS |

**The parkland around Arrow House is sure to be brimming with mushrooms when autumn comes around. This tart is substantial enough to provide a main for six people, or you could cut it into smaller slices and serve it as a starter for more.**

Roll out the pastry on a lightly floured surface to a disk about 3mm/⅛in thick. Sprinkle over half the thyme leaves and, using the rolling pin, gently press them into the dough.

Use the disk to line the tart tin, pressing the pastry into the base and corners and leaving a 2–3cm/¾–1¼in overhang. Chill the pastry case for 30 minutes to firm up. While the pastry case is chilling, preheat your oven to 180°C/160°C fan/350°F/Gas 4.

Trim the overhanging pastry and prick the base of the chilled pastry case all over with a fork. Line the pastry case with baking paper and fill it with baking beans or raw rice. Bake the case for about 15–20 minutes, then remove the paper and baking beans or rice and return it to the oven for a further 5–10 minutes, until lightly golden. Remove from the oven and leave to cool completely.

Melt half the butter in a medium saucepan over a medium heat. Add the chard stalks and a splash of water and cook for 5 minutes, until they have broken down. Add the chopped chard leaves to the pan and cook for 30 seconds to wilt. Remove the pan from the heat, leave the chard until cool enough to handle, then arrange the chard over the base of the cooled pastry case and scatter over the beetroot.

In a bowl, whisk together the eggs, cream, milk and Parmesan, and season with salt and pepper. Pour the mixture into the pastry case to cover the vegetables. Bake the tart for 40–45 minutes, until puffed up and golden.

Meanwhile, melt the remaining butter in a frying pan over a medium heat. Add the mushrooms and fry for 7–10 minutes, until softened. Add the garlic, walnuts and remaining thyme leaves and cook for 5 minutes, until the mushrooms have good colour. Remove the pan from the heat. Add the watercress, leaving the chopped leaves to wilt a little in the heat of the pan. Season with salt and pepper. Top the tart with the mushroom mixture and a few watercress leaves, then serve in slices.

# RACK OF LAMB WITH A MUSTARD & WHISKEY GLAZE & CAPER SAUCE

2 tablespoons olive oil
3 racks of lamb, French trimmed
    (ask your butcher to do this)
3 rosemary sprigs, leaves
    picked and chopped
3 garlic cloves, crushed
2 tablespoons Irish whiskey
1 tablespoon runny honey
2 tablespoons wholegrain mustard
salt and ground black pepper
steamed green beans and
    buttery peas, to serve
rosemary roasted potatoes,
    to serve

## FOR THE SAUCE

a knob of butter
2⅓ tablespoons plain
    (all-purpose) flour
300ml/10½fl oz/1¼ cups
    lamb stock
150ml/5fl oz/⅔ cup double
    (heavy) cream
2 tablespoons capers
1 teaspoon mint sauce

**Although the era would have meant the chefs were more likely to serve up hogget or mutton at the Arrow House dinner table, this recipe uses a prime cut of lamb, the 'best end', with its more subtle flavour. Eat it pink to keep the texture perfectly tender.**

Preheat your oven to 200°C/180°C fan/400°F/Gas 6. Place a large frying pan over a high heat.

Rub the olive oil all over the lamb and season generously with salt and pepper. Seal the lamb in the hot frying pan until browned all over (the ends, too!) – the darker, the better for flavour. Remove the lamb from the pan and place the racks into a roasting tin.

In a bowl, mix the rosemary with the garlic, whiskey, honey and mustard to create a marinade. Brush the marinade all over the lamb. Roast the lamb in the oven for 10–12 minutes. Remove the lamb from the oven and leave it to rest for 10 minutes.

While the lamb is resting, make the sauce. Melt the butter in a small saucepan over a medium heat. Stir in the flour, then add half the lamb stock. Stir until smooth. Add the remaining stock, stir to combine, then bring the liquid to a simmer. Add the cream, capers and mint sauce and season to taste. Pour the sauce into a warm jug.

Once the lamb has rested, carve it, serving 3 cutlets (half a rack) per person. Pour over the caper sauce and serve with a bowl of steamed green beans and buttery peas, and rosemary roasted potatoes.

SERVES 6 | TOTAL TIME TO MAKE 00 HOURS 35 MINS

# BUTTER & SAGE ROAST CHICKEN WITH MUSHROOMS & TARRAGON CREAM SAUCE

1 large chicken (about 1.25kg/2lb 12oz)
50g/1¾oz/3½ tablespoons
   butter, softened
10 sage leaves, chopped
a handful of flat-leaf parsley,
   leaves picked and chopped
4 garlic cloves, chopped
12 shallots, halved
5 rashers of smoked streaky bacon,
   chopped into chunky pieces
300g/10½oz chestnut
   mushrooms, sliced
200ml/7fl oz/generous
   ¾ cup dry white wine
300ml/10½fl oz/1¼ cups
   chicken stock
200ml/7fl oz/generous ¾ cup
   double (heavy) cream
5 tarragon sprigs, leaves picked
   and chopped, plus extra to serve
1 tablespoon cornflour (cornstarch)
salt and ground black pepper
steamed seasonal vegetables,
   to serve
roasted new potatoes, to serve

SERVES | TOTAL TIME TO MAKE
6 | 02 HOURS | 15 MINS

**In the early part of the 20th century, chicken was considered a luxury meat. The herby butter between the skin and the meat gives this roast chicken an intense and irresistible flavour.**

Preheat your oven to 180°C/160°C fan/350°F/Gas 4 and place the chicken into a large, heavy-based roasting tin.

In a small bowl, combine the butter, sage, parsley and garlic, and season with salt and pepper.

Using your fingers, loosen the chicken skin away from the breast, trying not to break the skin. Push most of the butter under the skin, pressing to make sure it's smooth and covering all the breast. Rub the remaining butter all over the outside of the chicken, season with salt and pepper, and roast for about 1½ hours, basting a few times during roasting, until the juices run clear when you make a cut between the breast and the leg. Remove the chicken from the roasting tin, loosely cover it with foil and leave it to rest on a warm plate while you make the sauce.

Place the roasting tin over a medium heat, add the shallots and smoked bacon and cook for 7–10 minutes, until the bacon starts to crisp and the shallots are golden. Add the mushrooms and cook for 3–4 minutes, until the mushrooms are coloured. Pour in the wine and leave to bubble away for a few minutes. Add the chicken stock and simmer for 10 minutes, then stir in the cream and tarragon and any rested chicken juices. Season to taste.

Mix the cornflour with 1 tablespoon of water to make a paste and stir half the paste into the sauce to thicken. If you want a thicker sauce, keep adding the cornflour paste, stirring over the heat, until you are happy with the consistency. Pour the sauce into a serving platter, then carve the chicken and place the meat on top. Scatter with a little extra tarragon and serve with seasonal vegetables and roasted new potatoes.

# VANILLA CUSTARD TART WITH ROASTED GOOSEBERRIES

1 x 500g/1lb 2oz block
    of shortcrust pastry
plain (all-purpose) flour,
    for dusting
4 eggs, beaten
400ml/14fl oz/1¾ cups
    double (heavy) cream
200ml/7fl oz/generous ¾ cup
    full-fat milk
2 teaspoons vanilla extract
2 egg yolks
160g/5¾oz/generous ¾ cup
    caster (superfine) sugar
a generous grating of nutmeg
300g/10½oz/generous
    2½ cups gooseberries
single (light) cream, to serve

You will need a 23cm/9in
loose-bottomed tart tin,
greased with a little butter.

SERVES | TOTAL TIME TO MAKE
10 | 02 HOURS | 00 MINS

**This tart has all the makings of a quintessential English dessert – gooseberries have been grown as food here since the 13th century.**

Roll out the pastry on a lightly floured surface to a disk about 5mm/¼in thick and slightly larger in diameter than the tart tin. Carefully lay the pastry over the tin. Tear off a small piece of pastry and use it to gently push the pastry into the bottom of the tin, across the base, into the corners and then up the inside, leaving a 2–3cm/¾–1¼in overhang. Chill the case for 20 minutes to firm up. Meanwhile, preheat your oven to 180°C/160°C fan/350°F/Gas 4.

Trim the pastry overhang and put the chilled, lined tart tin on a baking sheet and prick the base all over with a fork. Line the pastry case with baking paper and fill it with baking beans or raw rice. Bake the case for 15 minutes, then remove it from the oven and remove the baking beans or rice and baking paper. Brush the inside of the case with beaten egg and return it to the oven for 10 minutes, until golden. Leave it to cool completely. Reduce the oven to 140°C/120°C fan/275°F/Gas 1.

Pour the cream and milk into a medium saucepan and add the vanilla. Place the pan over a medium heat and bring the milk mixture to a simmer, then immediately remove it from the heat.

In a large mixing bowl, whisk together the remaining beaten egg, the egg yolks and 140g/5oz/scant ¾ cup of the sugar. Whisking continuously, gradually pour the warm milk mixture over the eggs until fully combined. Pour the mixture through a fine sieve into a jug and skim off any foamy bubbles that settle on the surface.

Place the pastry case on to the middle shelf of the oven, making sure it's level. Carefully pour the custard into the pastry case in the oven, sprinkle over the nutmeg and bake for about 1 hour, until just set with only the slightest wobble in the middle. Leave the tart to cool in the tin (about 1 hour), then remove it from the tin and place it in the fridge to set (about 2 hours).

Just before you're ready to serve, preheat the oven to 180°C/160°C fan/350°F/Gas 4. Place the gooseberries on a baking tray and sprinkle over the remaining sugar. Bake for about 10 minutes, until softened. Arrange the softened, warm gooseberries on top of the tart, then slice it and serve it with the cream. Any leftover tart will keep for up to 3 days in the fridge.

# SUMMER PUDDING WITH GIN-INFUSED BERRIES

150g/5½oz raspberries
150g/5½oz strawberries, sliced
150g/5½oz redcurrants
150g/5½oz pitted cherries, sliced
150g/5½oz blueberries
125g/4½oz/scant ⅔ cup
    caster (superfine) sugar
juice of 1 lemon
8 slices of white bread,
    crusts removed
2–3 tablespoons gin
whipped cream or crème
    fraîche, to serve

You will need a 1 litre/35fl oz heatproof
pudding bowl lined with cling film,
leaving a generous overhang.

| SERVES | TOTAL TIME TO MAKE | |
|---|---|---|
| 6 | 00 HOURS | 25 MINS |

**Adding a splash of gin to the berries in this pudding accentuates their flavour – and somehow makes it a particularly fitting end to a feast at Arrow House. Feel free to leave the gin out, though, for an alcohol-free version.**

Place all the fruit into a wide saucepan or frying pan. Sprinkle over the sugar and add the lemon juice. Place the pan over a low heat and bring the liquid to a simmer. Cook for 3–4 minutes, until everything is juicy. Remove from the heat and leave to cool.

Cut a disk of bread from one slice to perfectly fit the base of the pudding bowl. Dip the disk into the juices in the pan and position it, dipped side down, into the bottom of the bowl.

Set aside 1 remaining slice of bread and cut the rest of the slices in half. Dip the halved slices into the berry juice and use these to completely line the inside of the pudding bowl, overlapping each slice, facing the dipped sides outwards and leaving a slight overhang over the rim of the bowl. Set aside.

Stir the gin into the remaining juiciness in the pan. Spoon this into the lined bowl, gently pressing it down to pack in the fruit.

Cut the last slice of bread into a disk large enough to cover the fruit and place this on top. Bring the overhanging bread slices up and over the bread lid and bring up the cling film to seal in the bread and berries. Place a small plate or saucer on top of the pudding (it should have contact with the pudding, not the bowl) and place a weight (such as a can of beans) on top of the plate. Transfer the bowl (and weight) to a large plate to catch any leaky juices and place the pudding in the fridge overnight to firm up.

To serve, unwrap the cling film and place a serving plate over the top of the bowl. Invert the pudding out on to the serving plate and release it by gently holding the cling film as you lift the bowl away. Serve with whipped cream or crème fraîche.

# INDEX

Brimming with creative inspiration, how-to projects, and useful information to enrich your everyday life, quarto.com is a favourite destination for those pursuing their interests and passions.

Text and food photography © 2022 Quarto Publishing Plc
Stills and quotes from the Peaky Blinders Series © 2013–2022 Caryn Mandabach Productions.
Peaky Blinders™ © 2013–2022 Caryn Mandabach Productions Ltd. Licensed by Banijay Group.
Peaky Blinders is a registered trademark of Caryn Mandabach Productions Ltd. Licensed by Banijay Brands Limited.

First published in 2022 by White Lion Publishing
an imprint of The Quarto Group.
The Old Brewery, 6 Blundell Street
London, N7 9BH,
United Kingdom
T (0)20 7700 6700
www.QuartoKnows.com

A catalogue record for this book is available from the British Library.

ISBN 978-0-7112-7630-7
Ebook ISBN 978-0-7112-7631-4

10 9 8 7 6 5 4 3 2 1

Recipe Writer and Food Stylist: Rob Morris
Food Assistants: George Stocks & Hattie Baker
Food Photographer: Jamie Orlando Smith
Series Stills Photographer: Robert Viglasky
Design & Art Direction: Smith & Gilmour
Project Editor: Judy Barratt
Prop Stylist: Hannah Wilkinson
Publisher: Jessica Axe
Printed by GPS Group in Bosnia and Herzegovina

Cook's Notes:
Use medium-size vegetables, fruit and eggs, unless otherwise specified.
Use fish from sustainable sources, and organic meat, vegetables and fruit.
Use fresh herbs, unless otherwise specified.
Total make times are approximate and do not include downtime or 'waiting' time.
Use metric or imperial measurements, but not a mixture of both.

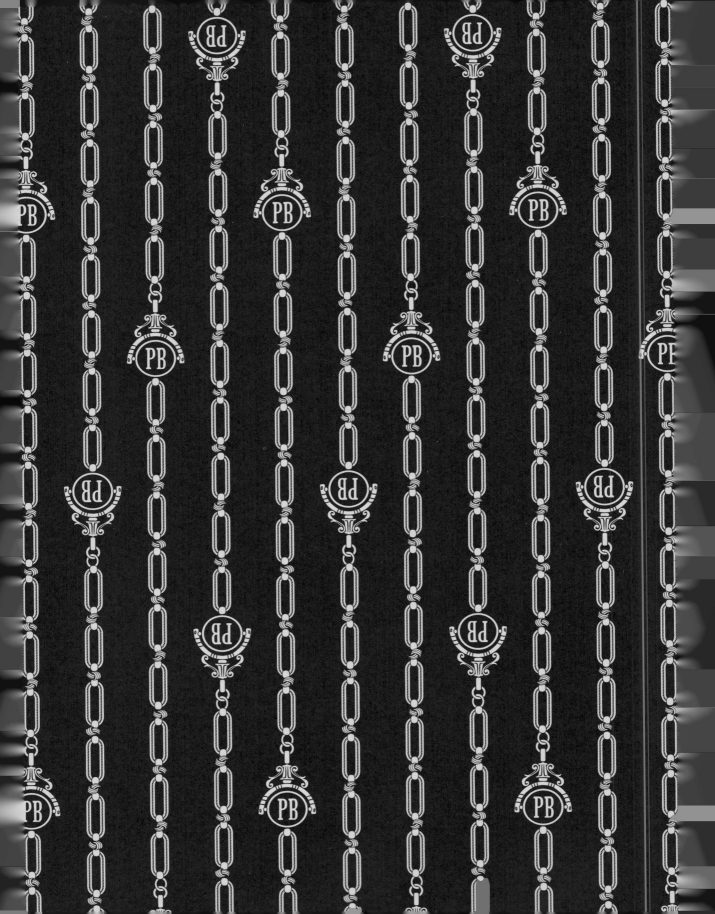